The ELEMENTS

The ELEM

ENTS

DAN GREEN

SCHOLASTIC discover more™

How to discover more

This book is very simple to use and enjoy, but by knowing a little bit more about the way it works, you will be able to discover more about elements and the parts of them that interest you most. Have a great read!

How the pages work

The book is divided into chapters, such as **Non-metals and gases**. Each chapter is made up of stand-alone spreads (double pages) that focus on specific topics.

Spread heading
The title of the spread lets you know what the subject is.

Fact boxes
Some spreads include a profile box with details about a specific element.

Element info
Coloured boxes give the atomic number of an element, its symbol, and its name.

Introduction
Most spreads have a general introduction to the subject.

Fantastic facts
BIG text gives an amazing fact or quote!

History of discovery
From cave paintings to carbon nanotubes, the last section of this book (pages 98–105) tracks elemental discoveries through the centuries.

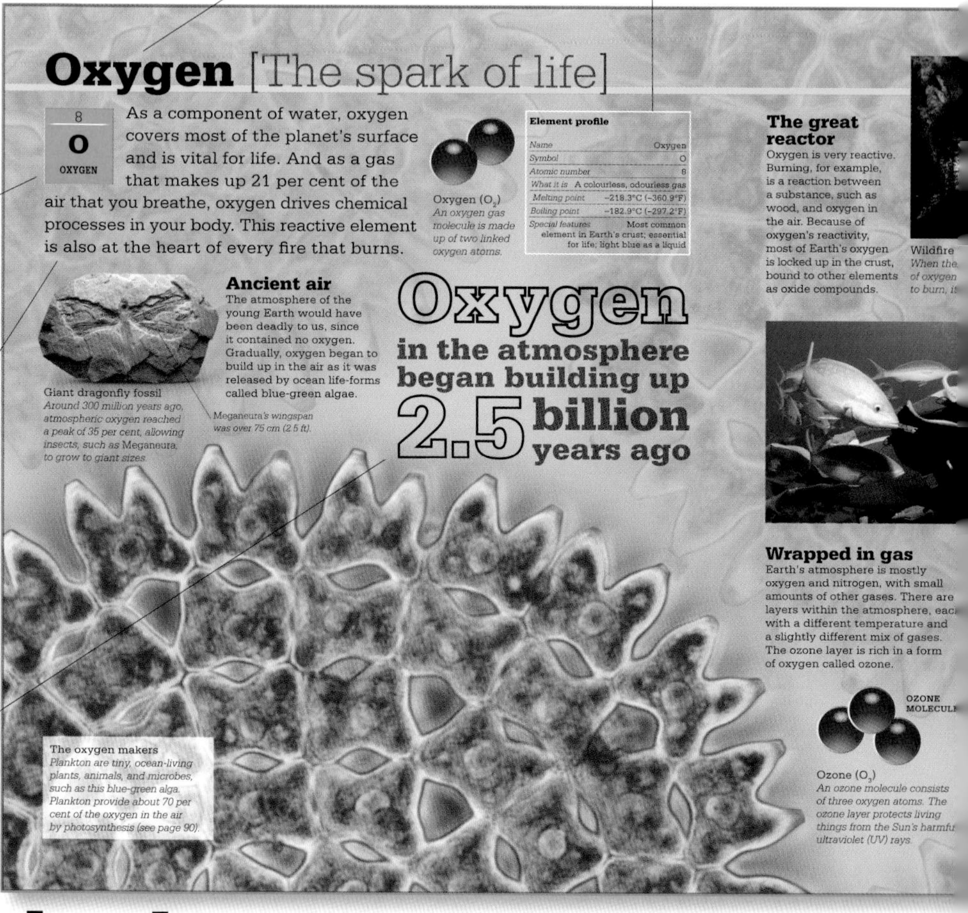

Oxygen [The spark of life]
8
O
OXYGEN
As a component of water, oxygen covers most of the planet's surface and is vital for life. And as a gas that makes up 21 per cent of the air that you breathe, oxygen drives chemical processes in your body. This reactive element is also at the heart of every fire that burns.
Oxygen (O_2)
An oxygen gas molecule is made up of two linked oxygen atoms.
Element profile
Name Oxygen
Symbol O
Atomic number 8
What it is A colourless, odourless gas
Melting point −218.3°C (−360.9°F)
Boiling point −182.9°C (−297.2°F)
Special features Most common element in Earth's crust; essential for life; light blue as a liquid
The great reactor
Oxygen is very reactive. Burning, for example, is a reaction between a substance, such as wood, and oxygen in the air. Because of oxygen's reactivity, most of Earth's oxygen is locked up in the crust, bound to other elements as oxide compounds.
Ancient air
The atmosphere of the young Earth would have been deadly to us, since it contained no oxygen. Gradually, oxygen began to build up in the air as it was released by ocean life-forms called blue-green algae.
Giant dragonfly fossil
Around 300 million years ago, atmospheric oxygen reached a peak of 35 per cent, allowing insects, such as Meganeura, to grow to giant sizes.
Meganeura's wingspan was over 75 cm (2.5 ft).
Oxygen in the atmosphere began building up 2.5 billion years ago
Wrapped in gas
Earth's atmosphere is mostly oxygen and nitrogen, with small amounts of other gases. There are layers within the atmosphere, each with a different temperature and a slightly different mix of gases. The ozone layer is rich in a form of oxygen called ozone.
OZONE MOLECULE
Ozone (O_3)
An ozone molecule consists of three oxygen atoms. The ozone layer protects living things from the Sun's harmful ultraviolet (UV) rays.
The oxygen makers
Plankton are tiny, ocean-living plants, animals, and microbes, such as this blue-green alga. Plankton provide about 70 per cent of the oxygen in the air by photosynthesis (see page 90).

Digital companion book

Download your free all-new digital book:

Elements Collector

Log on to

www.scholastic.com/discovermore

Enter your unique code:
RXKXX4247M2X

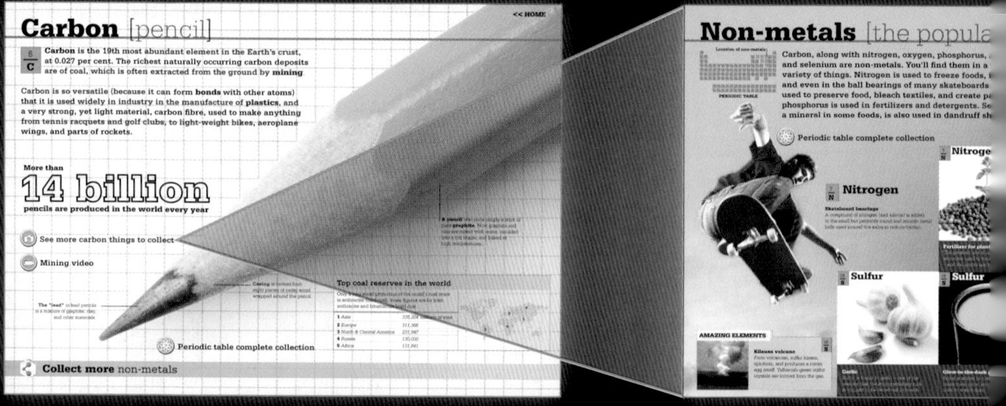

Carbon [pencil]
Carbon is the 19th most abundant element in the Earth's crust, at 0.027 per cent. The richest naturally occurring carbon deposits are of coal, which is often extracted from the ground by mining
More than 14 billion pencils are produced in the world every year
See more carbon things to collect
Mining video
Top coal reserves in the world
Periodic table complete collection
Collect more non-metals
Non-metals
Nitrogen
Sulfur

Collect every element from the periodic table.

Click for great ideas for your collection.

More here columns

This feature suggests books to read, places to visit, experiments, key words, and things to do.

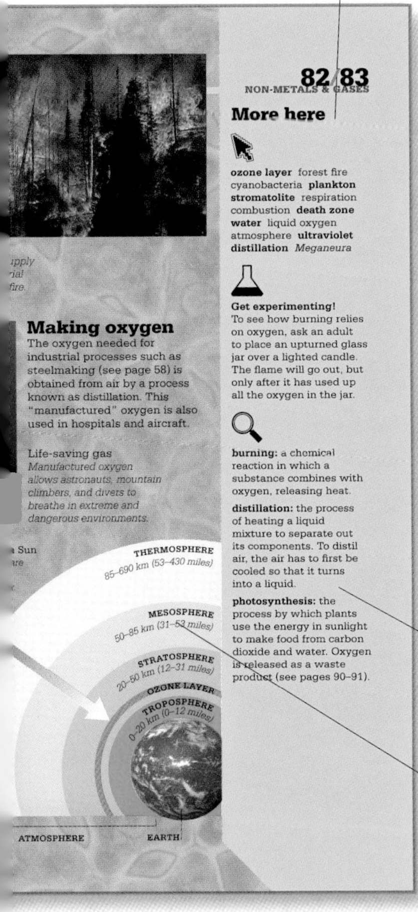
82/83
NON-METALS & GASES
More here
ozone layer forest fire cyanobacteria plankton stromatolite respiration combustion death zone water liquid oxygen atmosphere ultraviolet distillation Meganeura
Get experimenting!
To see how burning relies on oxygen, ask an adult to place an upturned glass jar over a lighted candle. The flame will go out, but only after it has used up all the oxygen in the jar.
burning: a chemical reaction in which a substance combines with oxygen, releasing heat.
distillation: the process of heating a liquid mixture to separate out its components. To distil air, the air has to first be cooled so that it turns into a liquid.
photosynthesis: the process by which plants use the energy in sunlight to make food from carbon dioxide and water. Oxygen is released as a waste product (see pages 90–91).
Making oxygen
The oxygen needed for industrial processes such as steelmaking (see page 58) is obtained from air by a process known as distillation. This "manufactured" oxygen is also used in hospitals and aircraft.
Life-saving gas
Manufactured oxygen allows astronauts, mountain climbers, and divers to breathe in extreme and dangerous environments.
THERMOSPHERE
85–690 km (53–430 miles)
MESOSPHERE
50–85 km (31–53 miles)
STRATOSPHERE
20–50 km (12–31 miles)
OZONE LAYER
TROPOSPHERE
0–20 km (0–12 miles)
ATMOSPHERE
EARTH

Spread types

Look out for different kinds of spreads such as catalogue spreads and feature spreads. There are also other spreads that are quite individual – that's what makes the book such fun to read of course.

Key to symbols in More here columns

- *Suggested reading*
- *Key words for web searches*
- *Fact file*
- *Experiment*
- *Mini glossary*
- *Places to visit*
- *View from afar*

Mini glossary

This explains difficult words and phrases you will find on the spread.

Identity labels

Many pictures have a label to tell you exactly what they are.

Alkaline earth metals [The upper-crust elements]
36/37
5th most common element in the oceans – magnesium
7 tonnes of ore is needed to produce just 1g (0.035oz) of radium

CATALOGUE SPREAD

Catalogue spread is packed full of information about a particular group of elements and their uses.

Copper [Old faithful]
64/65
The Statue of Liberty contains 81,000 kg of copper

FEATURE SPREAD

A timeline column gives you the most important dates on a topic.

PHOTOGRAPHIC SPREAD

This focuses in on an extraordinary subject, often providing an unfamiliar view, such as this worker in fireproof clothing in a blast furnace.

Glossary and index

The glossary explains words and phrases that might not be explained fully on the spread or in the **More here** column. The index can help you find the pages throughout the book on which words and topics appear.

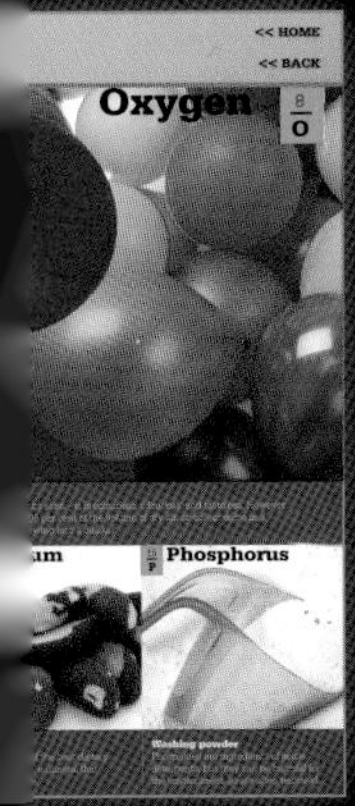
<< HOME
<< BACK
Oxygen
Phosphorus

Mining [digging deep]
Fast, modern conveyor belts shift
7,257 kg
of coal a minute from the mines

Read in-depth elements encyclopedia entries.

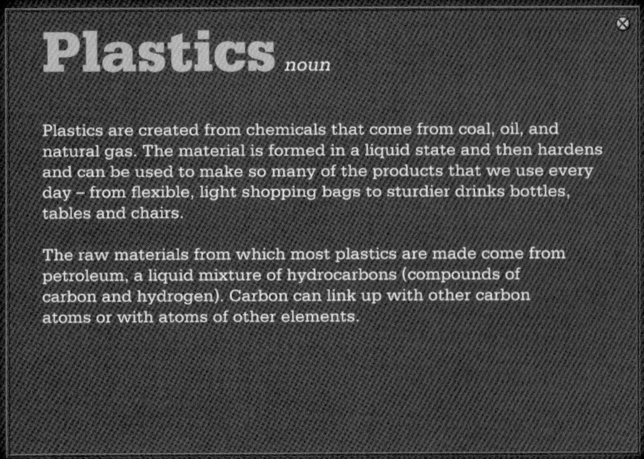
Plastics noun
Plastics are created from chemicals that come from coal, oil, and natural gas. The material is formed in a liquid state and then hardens and can be used to make so many of the products that we use every day – from flexible, light shopping bags to sturdier drinks bottles, tables and chairs.
The raw materials from which most plastics are made come from petroleum, a liquid mixture of hydrocarbons (compounds of carbon and hydrogen). Carbon can link up with other carbon atoms or with atoms of other elements.

Look up elements words.

Consultant: Dr Paul Lickiss, Department of Chemistry, Imperial College, London

Literacy consultant: Jane E. Mekkelsen, Literacy & Learning Connections LLC

Project editors: Steve Setford, Susan Malyan

Project art editor: Mark Lloyd

Designer: Clare Joyce

Art director: Bryn Walls

Managing editor: Miranda Smith

Cover designer: Natalie Godwin

DTP: John Goldsmid

Visual content editors: Alan Gottlieb, Dwayne Howard

Executive Director of Photography, Scholastic: Steve Diamond

"We must expect the discovery of many as yet unknown elements".

—DMITRI MENDELEEV

Library of Congress Cataloging-in-Publication Data Available
Distributed in the UK by Scholastic UK Ltd, Westfield Road, Southam, Warwickshire, England CV47 0RA

ISBN 978-1-407-13155-9

10 9 8 7 6 5 4 3 2 13 14 15 16

Printed in Singapore 46
First edition, March 2012

Scholastic is constantly working to lessen the environmental impact of our manufacturing processes. To view our industry-leading paper procurement policy, visit www.scholastic.com/paperpolicy.

Contents

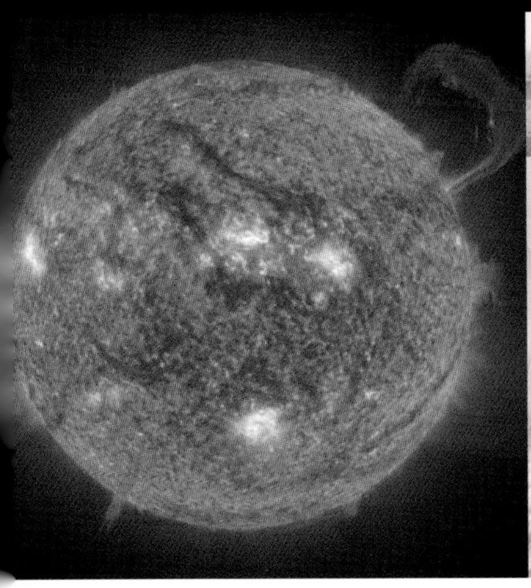

Meet the elements

Fiery & fizzing metals

Mainstream metals

Non-metals & gases

History of discovery

Crystal cave

Elements make up our world, and they can create awesome natural structures. Here, calcium (see pages 38–39), oxygen (see pages 82–83), and sulfur (see page 80) have combined to form vast crystals of selenite. The giant pillars – the world's largest known crystals – are up to 10 metres (33 feet) long and 50 tonnes in weight. They formed over 500,000 years from mineral-rich hot water that circulated through caverns in Chihuahua, Mexico.

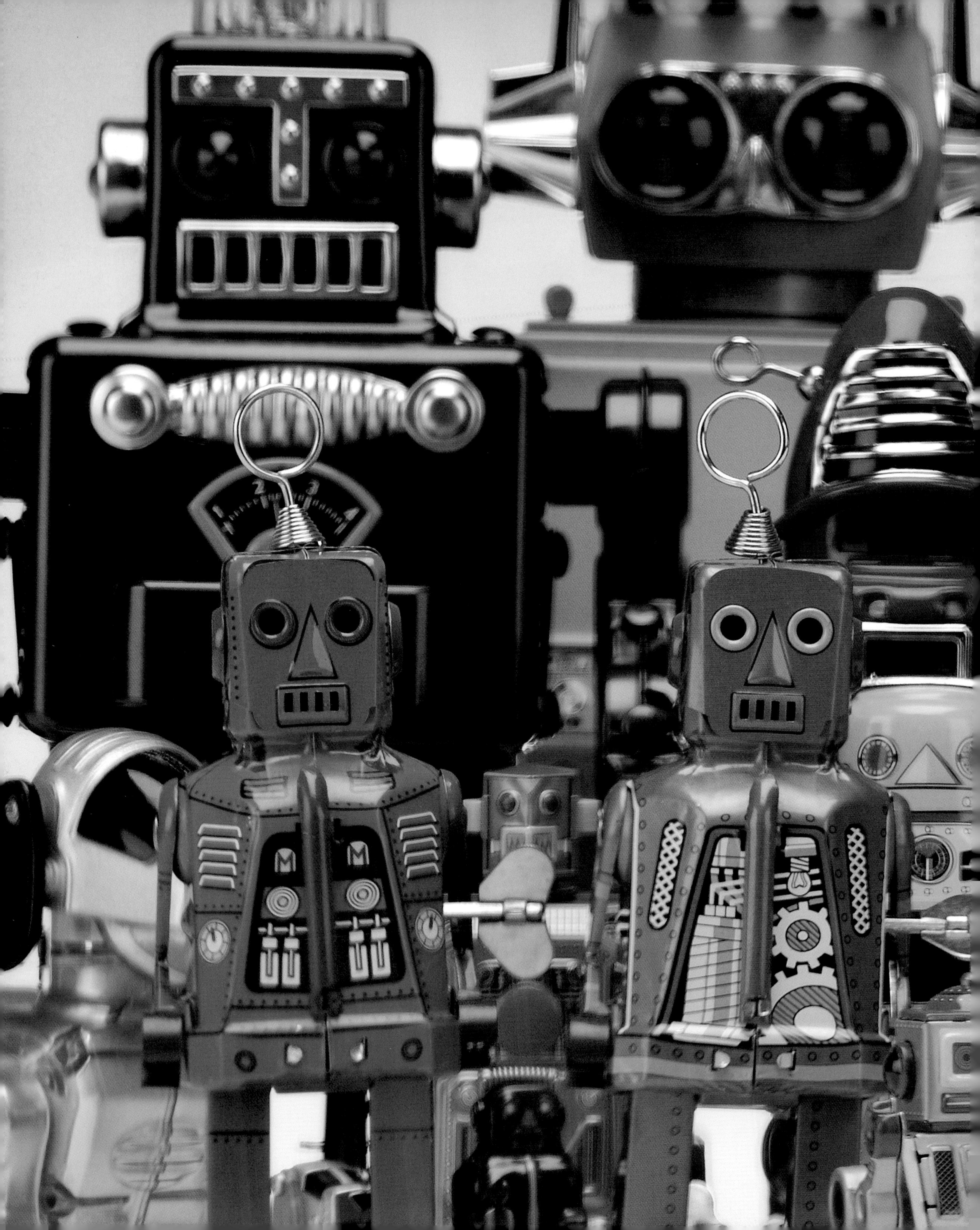

Robots on parade

One of the great things about elements is that we can combine and process them to make all sorts of fun stuff, such as these toy robots. Elements can be metals or non-metals. Most metals can be bent and shaped into any form you like, and many are super-durable, too. The bodies of these space-age robots are made from steel (see page 58) that has been given a thin coating of tin (see page 68). They are pressed into shape in moulds.

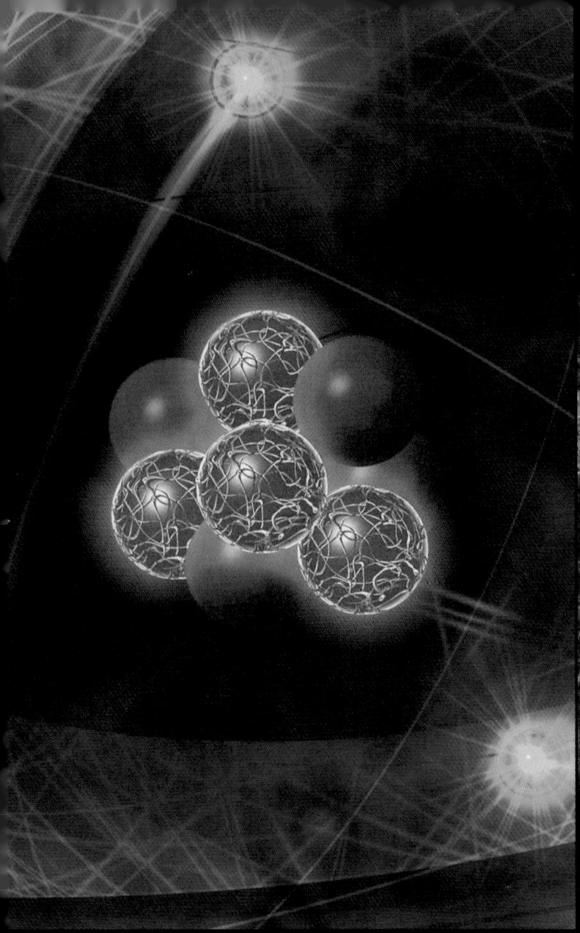

Meet
elem

-- What's inside a beryllium atom?

* Where do elements come from?

-- Who devised the periodic table of elements?

t the
ents

What is an element? [The

The stuff that's all around us is "matter" – from specks of dust and this book, to your phone, skyscrapers, and the Sun. Matter is made up of a mind-boggling number of combinations of 114 basic substances called elements. Only 92 elements occur naturally. The rest are synthetic – made by humans.

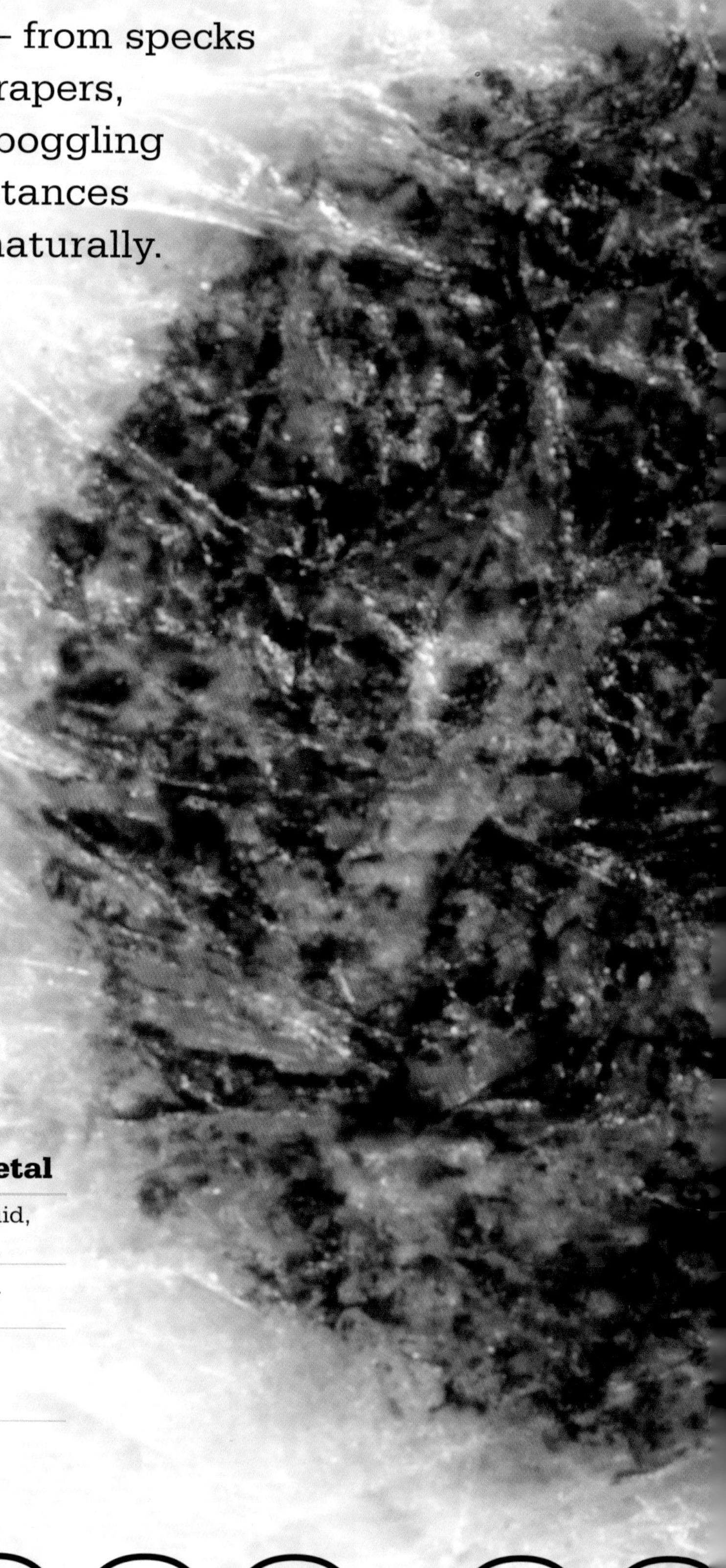

State of things

Elements are made up of tiny particles called atoms. Elements can exist in three states – solid, liquid, and gas. An element may change its state when the temperature or pressure alters.

A few elements change from solid to gas, and vice versa, without becoming liquid first.

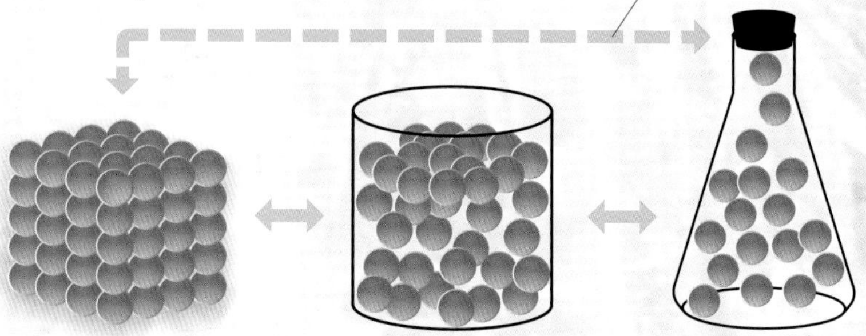

solid

A solid has a fixed, rigid shape. It will not flow or spread out. There are 101 solid elements.

liquid

A liquid can flow. It changes shape to fit its container. Only bromine and mercury are liquids.

gas

A gas can also flow, and it will always expand to fill its container. There are 11 gaseous elements.

What is it?

Most elements are either metals or non-metals. This chart shows you their different properties. A few elements, called metalloids, have both metal and non-metal properties.

Property	Metal	Non-metal
State at normal room temperature	Solid (except mercury)	Solid, liquid, or gas
Appearance: shiny or not shiny?	Shiny	Not shiny
Good or poor conductor of heat and electricity?	Good	Poor
Can it be beaten or stretched into shape without breaking?	Yes	No

9,500,000,00

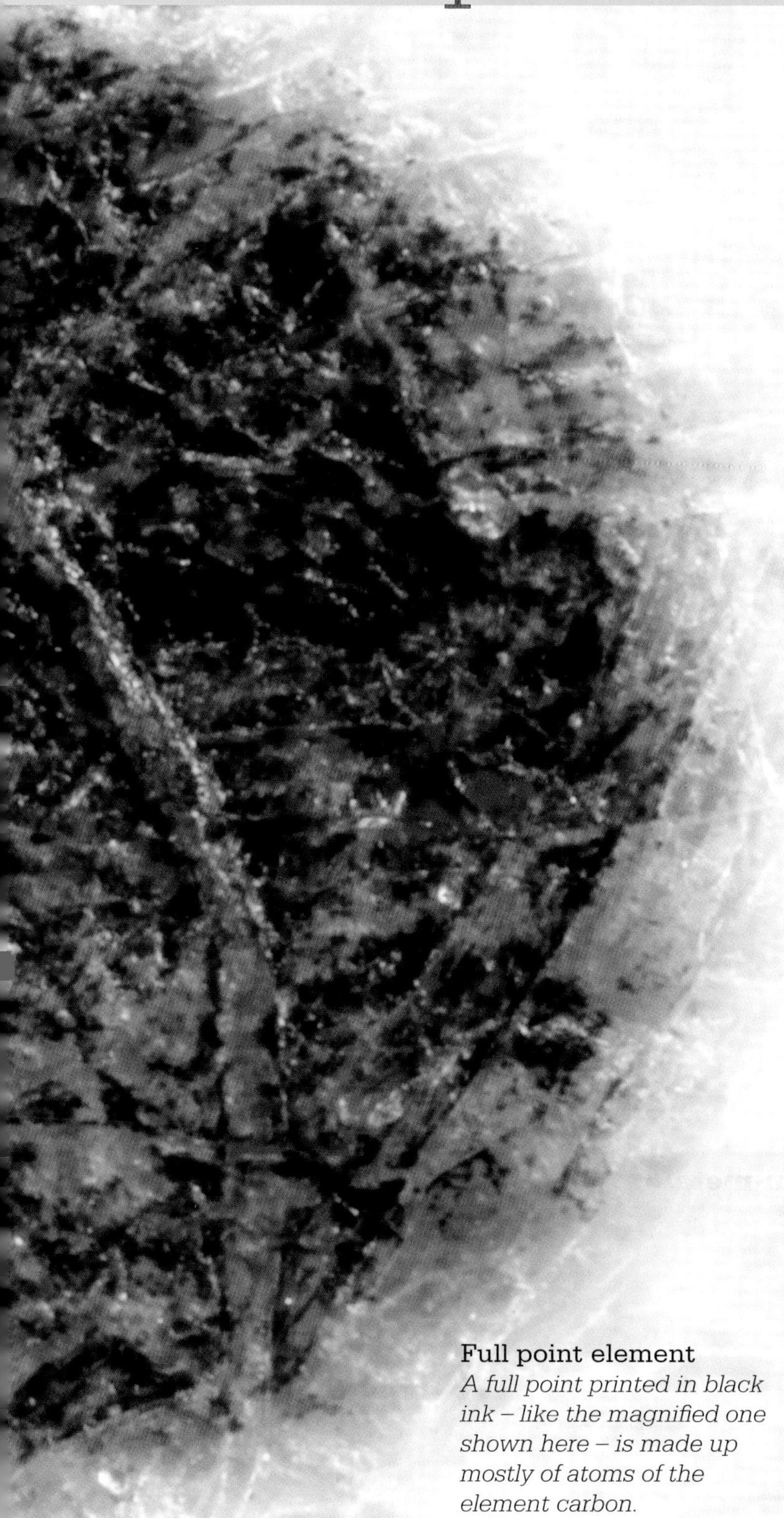

Making new substances

Elements can react, or combine, with one another to make new substances called compounds. Almost all the things around you right now are compounds. The properties of a compound can be very different from those of the elements from which it is made.

Making table salt
The elements sodium and chlorine combine to form the compound sodium chloride – table salt.

+

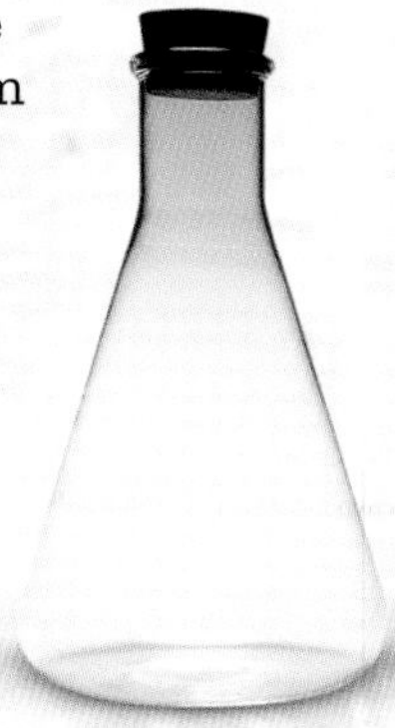

=

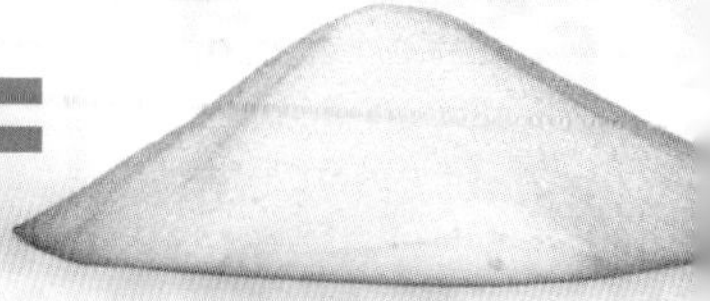

sodium

A shiny, soft metal, sodium reacts readily with other elements.

chlorine

Chlorine is a greenish gas that is poisonous in large quantities.

sodium chloride

Sodium chloride is an edible compound of white crystals.

Chemical reactions

Interactions between elements are called chemical reactions. Elements that are more prone than others to form new compounds are said to be reactive. Those that are less likely to interact are unreactive.

Reactive oxygen
Burning is a type of reaction between a substance and oxygen in the air, which releases lots of heat.

Full point element
A full point printed in black ink – like the magnified one shown here – is made up mostly of atoms of the element carbon.

0,000 **the number of atoms found in this full point** (at normal size) **from a daily newspaper**

Everyday elements [Car talk]

Don't be fooled into thinking that elements are found only in laboratories – they're the stuff of daily life! We use them for every product we make. Cars show how we can combine the qualities of different elements for the best result.

Early cars

From the first models, steel (a mixture of iron and a little carbon) took the lead role in cars. Steel is hard, strong, and easy to shape.

Ford Model T (1908–1927)
This early car was made mostly of steel, iron, and wood.

Perfect properties

Today's cars contain a wide range of elements and compounds. Many compounds are metallic, and metal mixtures called alloys are also used. Plastics (compounds of hydrogen, carbon, nitrogen, oxygen, and other elements) feature strongly.

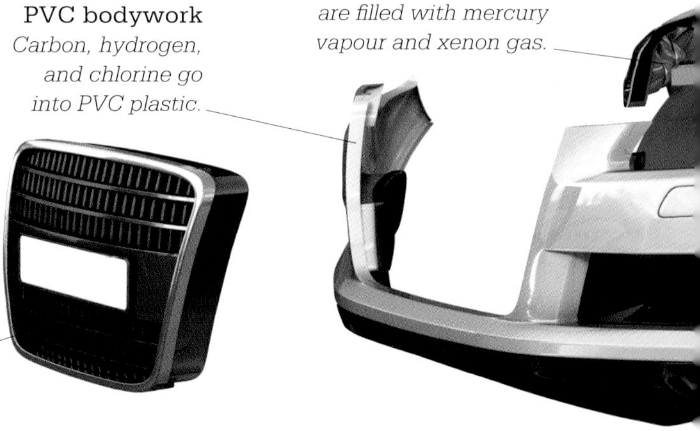

Headlight
Halogen headlights are filled with mercury vapour and xenon gas.
PVC bodywork
Carbon, hydrogen, and chlorine go into PVC plastic.
Radiator grill
PVC is moulded into complex shapes to make grills, fenders, and rearview mirrors.

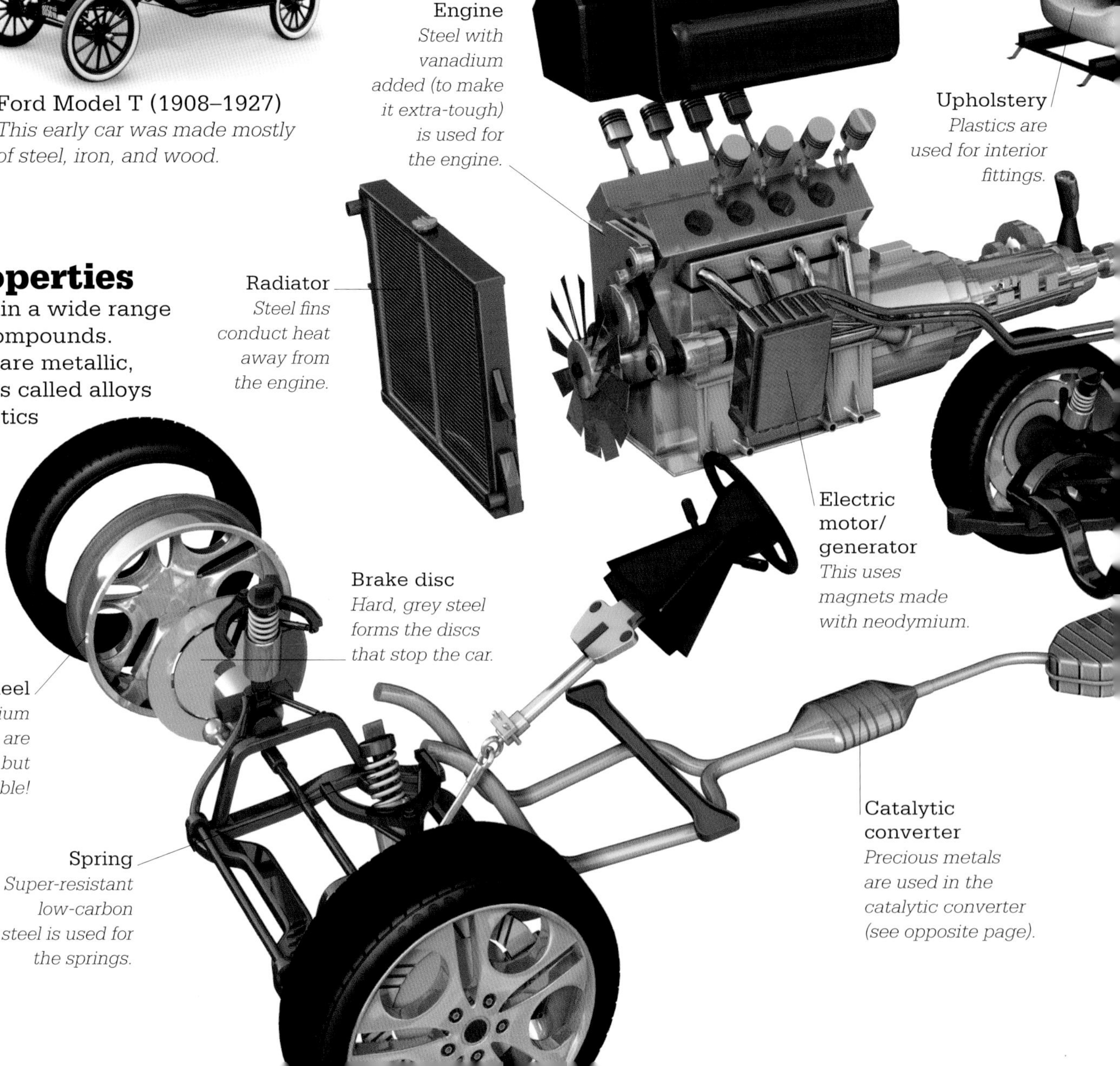

Engine
Steel with vanadium added (to make it extra-tough) is used for the engine.
Upholstery
Plastics are used for interior fittings.
Radiator
Steel fins conduct heat away from the engine.
Electric motor/ generator
This uses magnets made with neodymium.
Brake disc
Hard, grey steel forms the discs that stop the car.
Wheel
Magnesium alloy wheels are incredibly light – but also flammable!
Catalytic converter
Precious metals are used in the catalytic converter (see opposite page).
Spring
Super-resistant low-carbon steel is used for the springs.

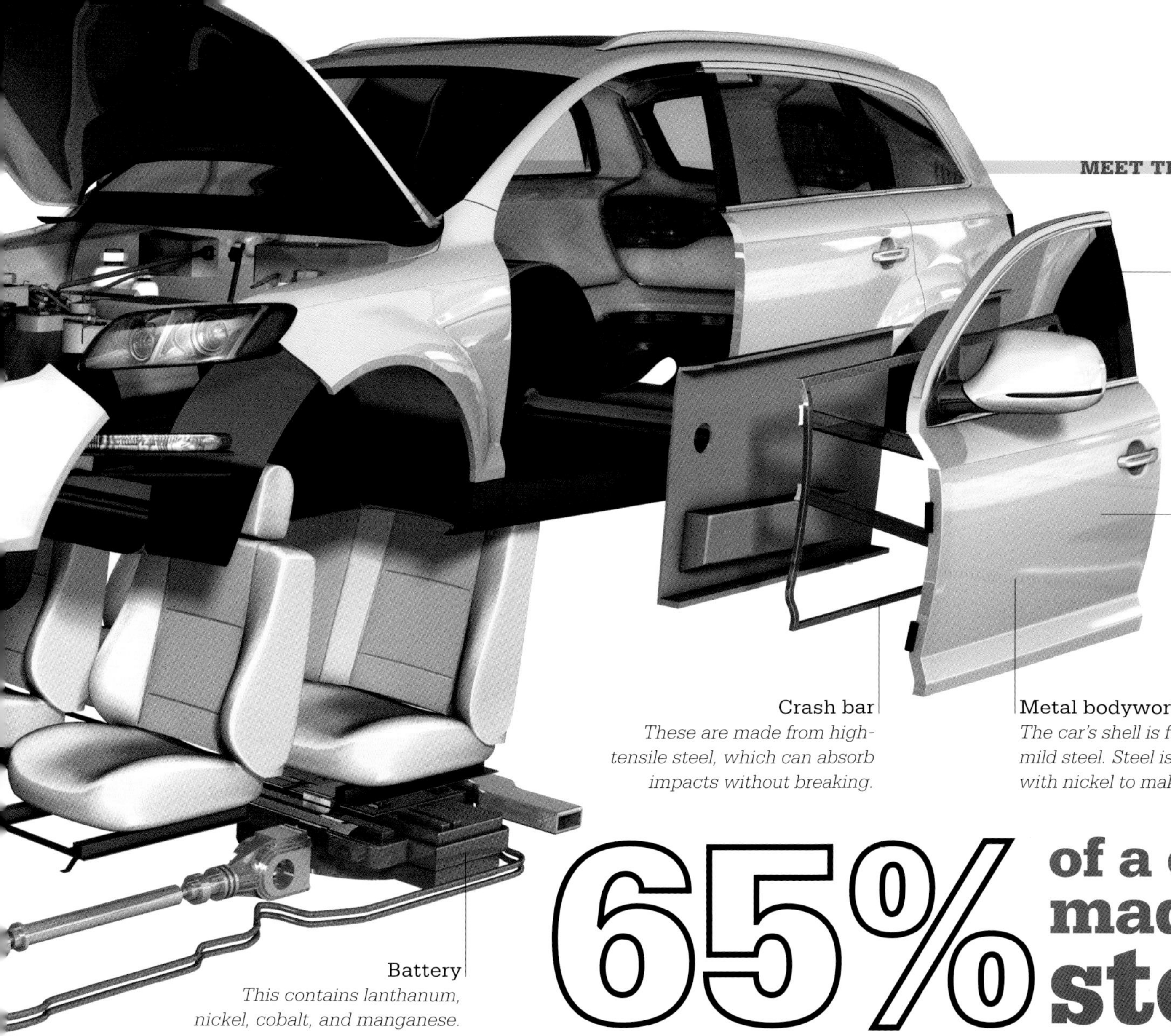

Window
Glass is made of silicon combined with oxygen.

Paintwork
Cadmium is often used in automobile paints.

Crash bar
These are made from high-tensile steel, which can absorb impacts without breaking.

Metal bodywork
The car's shell is formed from mild steel. Steel is often plated with nickel to make it shiny.

Battery
This contains lanthanum, nickel, cobalt, and manganese.

65% of a car is made of steel

Fuel tank
The tank is made of hard plastic.

Rubber tyre
Rubber is mainly carbon and hydrogen. In tyres, it is stiffened with sulfur and strengthened with steel wires.

Cleaning up

Inside a catalytic converter, chemical reactions turn polluting gases and unburned chemicals from petrol into less hazardous substances.

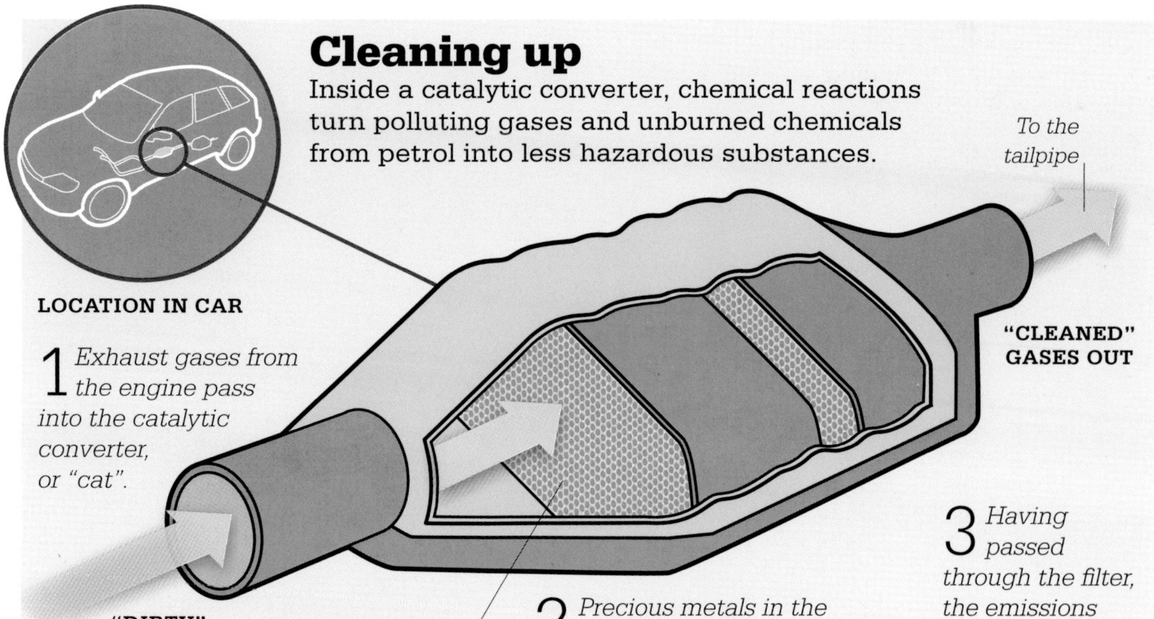
LOCATION IN CAR
To the tailpipe
"CLEANED" GASES OUT
"DIRTY" EXHAUST GASES IN
Ceramic filter has a thin coating of precious metals.

1 *Exhaust gases from the engine pass into the catalytic converter, or "cat".*

2 *Precious metals in the cat's ceramic filter, such as rhodium, platinum, and palladium, help the cleaning reactions take place.*

3 *Having passed through the filter, the emissions from the tailpipe are less harmful to people and the environment.*

Atoms [The building blocks

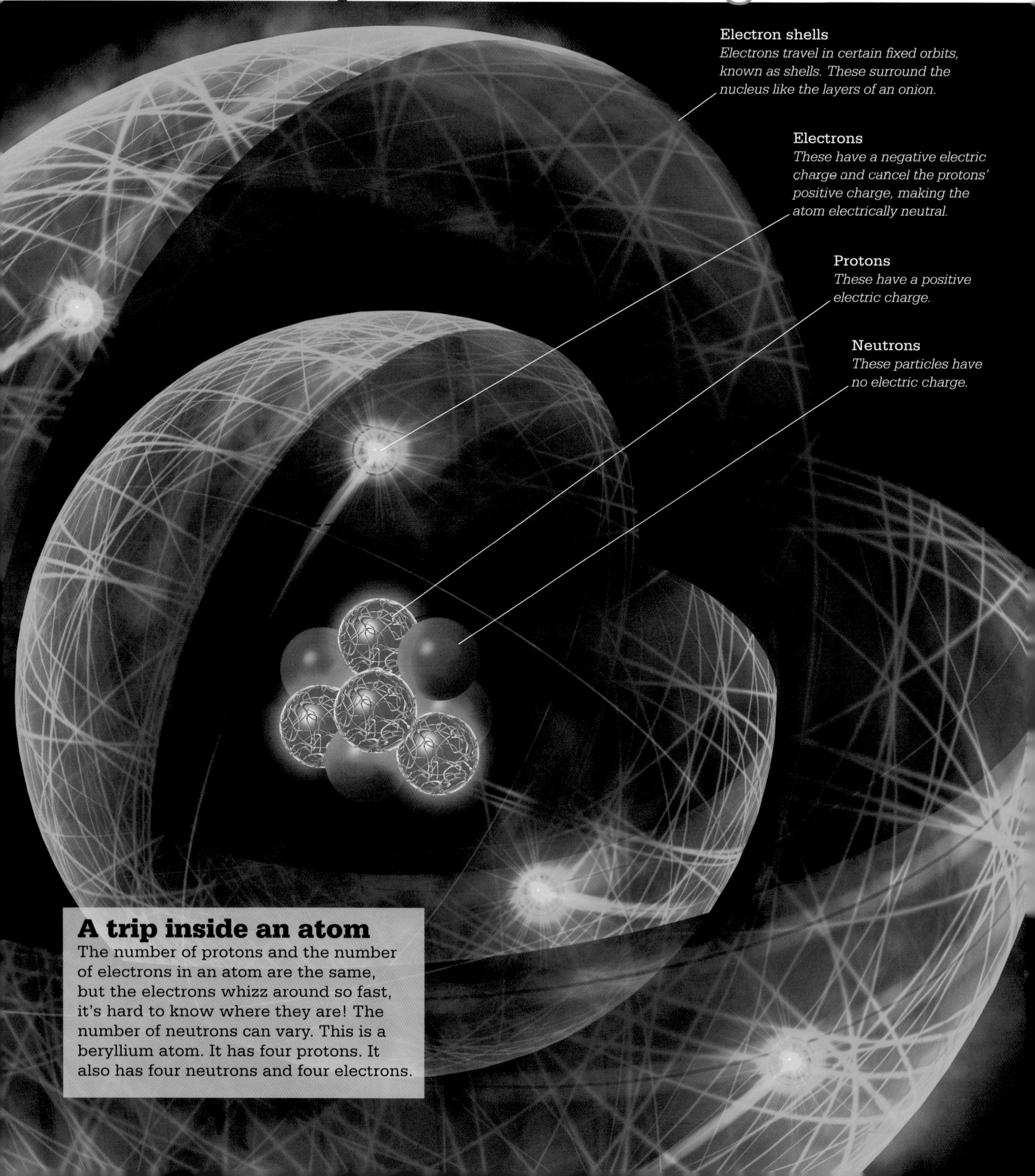
Electron shells
Electrons travel in certain fixed orbits, known as shells. These surround the nucleus like the layers of an onion.
Electrons
These have a negative electric charge and cancel the protons' positive charge, making the atom electrically neutral.
Protons
These have a positive electric charge.
Neutrons
These particles have no electric charge.

A trip inside an atom

The number of protons and the number of electrons in an atom are the same, but the electrons whizz around so fast, it's hard to know where they are! The number of neutrons can vary. This is a beryllium atom. It has four protons. It also has four neutrons and four electrons.

Every single thing in the Universe, including human beings, is made of tiny particles called atoms. Pure elements contain atoms of only one type. Compounds (see page 15) are combinations of more than one kind of atom, joined in units called molecules.

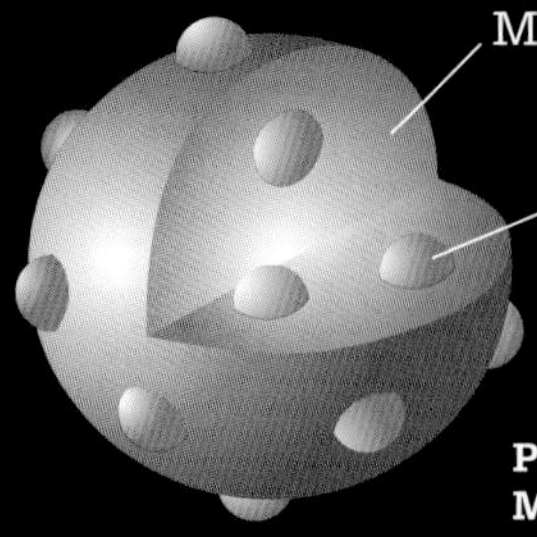
Mass of protons
Electron

PLUM PUDDING MODEL (1904)

99.9% of an atom's mass is in its nucleus

Getting the look

Scientists once thought that atoms might be all kinds of strange shapes. J. J. Thomson (1856–1940) suggested this "plum pudding" shape, in which the electrons were embedded in a mass of protons.

Atoms and elements

Atoms are made of even smaller stuff. A nucleus or central core contains protons and neutrons. Electrons orbit the nucleus. All atoms of the same element have an identical number of protons.

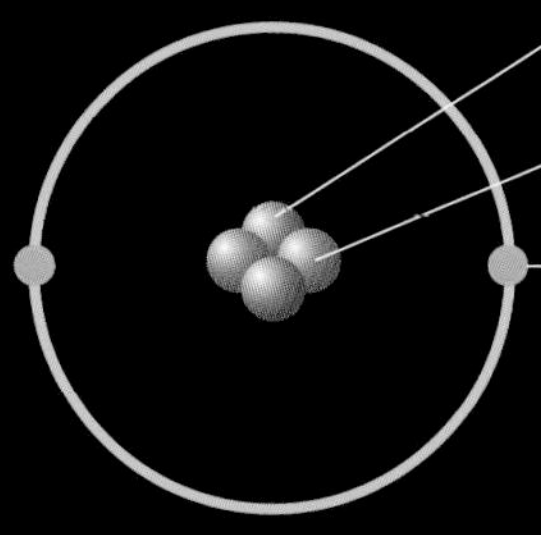
Proton
Neutron
Electron

Simple helium

Helium has simple atoms with two protons and two electrons. Helium is one of the most common elements in the Universe.

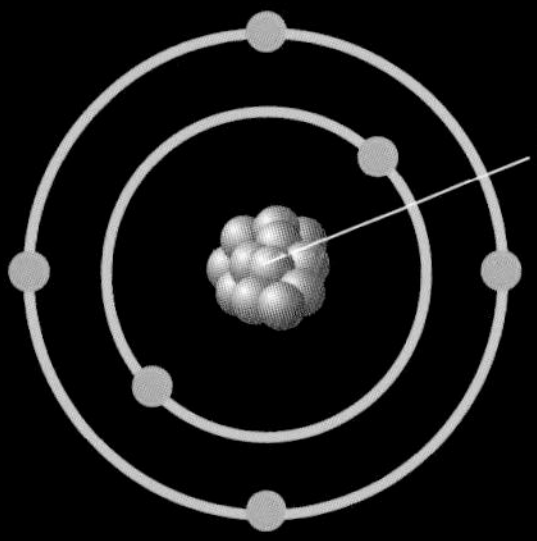
Nucleus

More complex carbon

A carbon atom has six protons and six electrons. Atoms can "steal" or "share" electrons to form bonds with other atoms.

Carbon
Oxygen

Molecules

Carbon dioxide is a compound of the elements carbon and oxygen. Its molecules have one carbon atom bonded (linked) to two oxygen atoms.

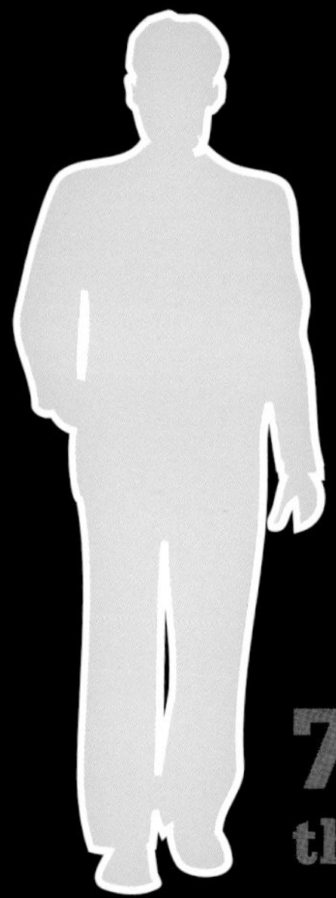

Smaller and smaller

There are even smaller particles than protons and neutrons. Machines called particle accelerators smash protons together at high speed, and scientists study the new particles that form during such collisions.

A real smasher

This is part of the world's largest particle accelerator, the Large Hadron Collider in Switzerland.

7,000,000,000,000,000,000,000,000,000: the number of atoms in an average human

Making elements [Where did

The story of the elements goes back to the beginning of time itself. The first three elements – the light gases hydrogen and helium and the metal lithium – were created soon after our Universe sprang into existence.

1 Big Bang
This explosion was probably the beginning of everything – time, space, and all the matter in the Universe. Within half an hour, single protons formed hydrogen nuclei, and two protons and two neutrons joined together to form helium nuclei.

From the stars

Scientists think that the Universe began about 13.7 billion years ago in an event called the Big Bang. This produced hydrogen, helium, and lithium. All the other elements formed much later, inside stars.

5 New worlds
Every time a star is formed and later dies, a cloud of stardust containing the elements is created, and new stars and planets form out of the debris of the supernova. Rare and heavy elements are carried to planets around the Universe, such as Earth, by meteorites.

99%
of everything in the Universe is just two elements – hydrogen and helium

they come from?]

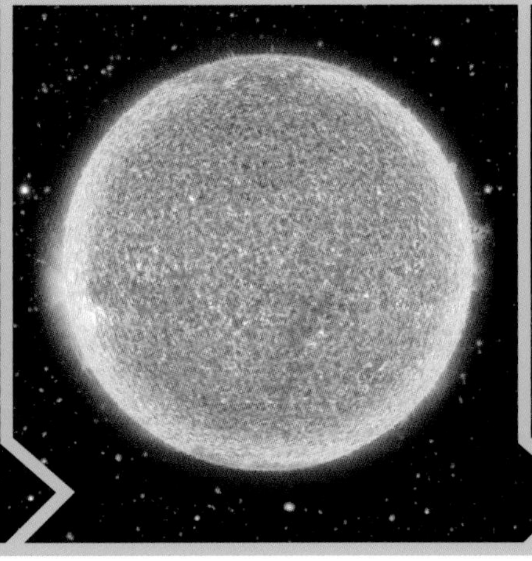

2 Birth of a star
Hydrogen atoms form vast clouds called nebulae. These collapse, getting hotter and making new stars form. The huge amount of energy released makes the stars shine brightly.

3 Burned out
A star fuses hydrogen atoms together to make helium. When it runs out of hydrogen, it starts fusing helium to form carbon. This process continues, making heavier elements up to iron.

4 Supernova
At the end of its life, a massive star explodes as a supernova. The explosion's extreme temperature and pressure allow gold, uranium, and other elements heavier than iron to form.

More here

George's Cosmic Treasure Hunt by Lucy and Stephen Hawking
The Hitchhiker's Guide to the Galaxy by Douglas Adams

Big Bang Universe **Kepler's Supernova** Milky Way **Crab Nebula** Meteorite ALH84001 from Mars

Look at the stars through a telescope and see new elements in the making!

Visit the Smithsonian National Air and Space Museum, Washington, DC, USA.
Check out the Arecibo Observatory near Arecibo, Puerto Rico.

fusion: the process that creates a new element by joining the nuclei of atoms.

meteorite: a piece of space rock that lands on Earth.

nebula: a cloud of gas and dust in space.

supernova: a huge explosion that takes place when a star has used up all its fuel and collapses.

The periodic table [Sorting

The periodic table organizes all the elements according to their shared characteristics. This arrangement was devised in 1869 by Dmitri Mendeleev (see page 102), a Russian chemist. You can predict an element's "personality" – its properties and chemical behaviour – from its position in the table.

22 — Atomic number
Ti — Symbol
TITANIUM — Element name

A shining example
An element's atomic number shows how many protons there are in the nucleus (see page 18). Each element also has a unique symbol – normally one or two letters taken from its name.

Elements become less metallic in this direction.

GROUPS (VERTICAL COLUMNS)

PERIODS (HORIZONTAL ROWS)

	1	2	3	4	5	6	7	8	9	10
1	1 **H** HYDROGEN									
2	3 **Li** LITHIUM	4 **Be** BERYLLIUM								
3	11 **Na** SODIUM	12 **Mg** MAGNESIUM								
4	19 **K** POTASSIUM	20 **Ca** CALCIUM	21 **Sc** SCANDIUM	22 **Ti** TITANIUM	23 **V** VANADIUM	24 **Cr** CHROMIUM	25 **Mn** MANGANESE	26 **Fe** IRON	27 **Co** COBALT	28 **Ni** NICKEL
5	37 **Rb** RUBIDIUM	38 **Sr** STRONTIUM	39 **Y** YTTRIUM	40 **Zr** ZIRCONIUM	41 **Nb** NIOBIUM	42 **Mo** MOLYBDENUM	43 **Tc** TECHNETIUM	44 **Ru** RUTHENIUM	45 **Rh** RHODIUM	46 **Pd** PALLADIUM
6	55 **Cs** CAESIUM	56 **Ba** BARIUM	57–71 **La–Lu** LANTHANOIDS	72 **Hf** HAFNIUM	73 **Ta** TANTALUM	74 **W** TUNGSTEN	75 **Re** RHENIUM	76 **Os** OSMIUM	77 **Ir** IRIDIUM	78 **Pt** PLATINUM
7	87 **Fr** FRANCIUM	88 **Ra** RADIUM	89–103 **Ac–Lr** ACTINOIDS	104 **Rf** RUTHERFORDIUM	105 **Db** DUBNIUM	106 **Sg** SEABORGIUM	107 **Bh** BOHRIUM	108 **Hs** HASSIUM	109 **Mt** MEITNERIUM	110 **Ds** DARMSTADTIUM

With scandium and yttrium, the lanthanoids are together known as rare earth metals.

57 **La** LANTHANUM	58 **Ce** CERIUM	59 **Pr** PRASEODYMIUM	60 **Nd** NEODYMIUM	61 **Pm** PROMETHIUM	62 **Sm** SAMARIUM	63 **Eu** EUROPIUM
89 **Ac** ACTINIUM	90 **Th** THORIUM	91 **Pa** PROTACTINIUM	92 **U** URANIUM	93 **Np** NEPTUNIUM	94 **Pu** PLUTONIUM	95 **Am** AMERICIUM

3/4 of all known elements are metals

92 elements occur naturally on Earth, the rest are manufactured

Fluorine is the most reactive element.

Silicon is the second most abundant element in Earth's crust.

Silver is both the best conductor and the most reflective element.

11	12	13	14	15	16	17	18
							2 He HELIUM
		5 B BORON	6 C CARBON	7 N NITROGEN	8 O OXYGEN	9 F FLUORINE	10 Ne NEON
		13 Al ALUMINIUM	14 Si SILICON	15 P PHOSPHORUS	16 S SULFUR	17 Cl CHLORINE	18 Ar ARGON
29 Cu COPPER	30 Zn ZINC	31 Ga GALLIUM	32 Ge GERMANIUM	33 As ARSENIC	34 Se SELENIUM	35 Br BROMINE	36 Kr KRYPTON
47 Ag SILVER	48 Cd CADMIUM	49 In INDIUM	50 Sn TIN	51 Sb ANTIMONY	52 Te TELLURIUM	53 I IODINE	54 Xe XENON
79 Au GOLD	80 Hg MERCURY	81 Tl THALLIUM	82 Pb LEAD	83 Bi BISMUTH	84 Po POLONIUM	85 At ASTATINE	86 Rn RADON
111 Rg ROENTGENIUM	112 Cn COPERNICIUM		114 Uuq UNUNQUADIUM		116 Uuh UNUNHEXIUM		

Other elements
Elements 113, 115, 117, and 118 are awaiting official recognition and naming.

64 Gd GADOLINIUM	65 Tb TERBIUM	66 Dy DYSPROSIUM	67 Ho HOLMIUM	68 Er ERBIUM	69 Tm THULIUM	70 Yb YTTERBIUM	71 Lu LUTETIUM
96 Cm CURIUM	97 Bk BERKELIUM	98 Cf CALIFORNIUM	99 Es EINSTEINIUM	100 Fm FERMIUM	101 Md MENDELEVIUM	102 No NOBELIUM	103 Lr LAWRENCIUM

Team talk

The groups, or vertical columns, are families of elements that react in similar ways. Generally, the elements in a group become more reactive towards the bottom. Sometimes, similarities are also shared across neighbouring groups, forming larger teams of related elements.

Alkali metals
Soft, shiny, and extremely reactive metals.

Alkaline earth metals
Silvery-white reactive metals that form minerals.

Transition metals
Tough, versatile metals that are easy to shape.

Poor metals
Soft metals with some non-metal properties.

Metalloids
These have both metal and non-metal properties.

Non-metals
Gases and solids that vary in their chemistry.

Halogens
Group of reactive elements, also called salt-formers.

Noble gases
Generally unreactive, colourless, and odourless.

Lanthanoids
Reactive metals that have similar chemistry.

Actinoids
Many of these are made in nuclear reactors.

Gallery | The periodic table in

The periodic table lays out the elements in order of increasing atomic number. Solid metal elements fill up most of the table, while non-metals and gases cluster on the right-hand side. Not all the elements are pictured in this gallery. Some elements exist only briefly before they decay by radioactivity (see pages 64–65), so it is not possible to photograph them.

H 1 HYDROGEN								
Li 3 LITHIUM	Be 4 BERYLLIUM							
Na 11 SODIUM	Mg 12 MAGNESIUM							
K 19 POTASSIUM	Ca 20 CALCIUM	Sc 21 SCANDIUM	Ti 22 TITANIUM	V 23 VANADIUM	Cr 24 CHROMIUM	Mn 25 MANGANESE	Fe 26 IRON	Co 27 COBALT
Rb 37 RUBIDIUM	Sr 38 STRONTIUM	Y 39 YTTRIUM	Zr 40 ZIRCONIUM	Nb 41 NIOBIUM	Mo 42 MOLYBDENUM	Tc 43 TECHNETIUM	Ru 44 RUTHENIUM	Rh 45 RHODIUM
Cs 55 CAESIUM	Ba 56 BARIUM	57–71 La–Lu LANTHANOIDS	Hf 72 HAFNIUM	Ta 73 TANTALUM	W 74 TUNGSTEN	Re 75 RHENIUM	Os 76 OSMIUM	Ir 77 IRIDIUM
Fr 87 FRANCIUM	Ra 88 RADIUM	89–103 Ac–Lr ACTINOIDS	104 Rf RUTHERFORDIUM	105 Db DUBNIUM	106 Sg SEABORGIUM	107 Bh BOHRIUM	108 Hs HASSIUM	109 Mt MEITNERIUM

La 57 LANTHANUM	Ce 58 CERIUM	Pr 59 PRASEODYMIUM	Nd 60 NEODYMIUM	Pm 61 PROMETHIUM	Sm 62 SAMARIUM
Ac 89 ACTINIUM	Th 90 THORIUM	Pa 91 PROTACTINIUM	U 92 URANIUM	93 Np NEPTUNIUM	Pu 94 PLUTONIUM

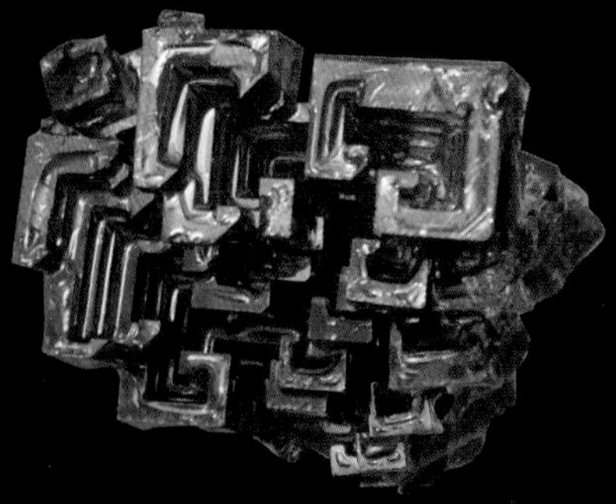

Bismuth (83)
When this element cools from a molten state, it forms unusual square spiral shapes.

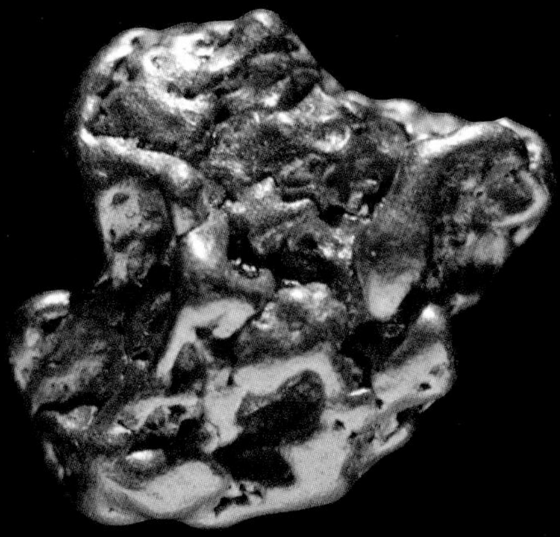

Gold (79)
Many elements are extremely reactive, meaning that they combine readily with other elements. Precious metals, such as gold, are both rare and highly unreactive.

Some gases are naturally colourless but glow when electricity passes through them.

								He 2 HELIUM
			B 5 BORON	C 6 CARBON	N 7 NITROGEN	O 8 OXYGEN	F 9 FLUORINE	Ne 10 NEON
			Al 13 ALUMINIUM	Si 14 SILICON	P 15 PHOSPHORUS	S 16 SULFUR	Cl 17 CHLORINE	Ar 18 ARGON
Ni 28 NICKEL	Cu 29 COPPER	Zn 30 ZINC	Ga 31 GALLIUM	Ge 32 GERMANIUM	As 33 ARSENIC	Se 34 SELENIUM	Br 35 BROMINE	Kr 36 KRYPTON
Pd 46 PALLADIUM	Ag 47 SILVER	Cd 48 CADMIUM	In 49 INDIUM	Sn 50 TIN	Sb 51 ANTIMONY	Te 52 TELLURIUM	I 53 IODINE	Xe 54 XENON
Pt 78 PLATINUM	Au 79 GOLD	Hg 80 MERCURY	Tl 81 THALLIUM	Pb 82 LEAD	Bi 83 BISMUTH	Po 84 POLONIUM	At 85 ASTATINE	Rn 86 RADON
110 Ds DARMSTADTIUM	111 Rg ROENTGENIUM	112 Cn COPERNICIUM		114 Uuq UNUNQUADIUM		116 Uuh UNUNHEXIUM	Other elements *Elements 113, 115, 117, and 118 are awaiting official recognition.*	

Eu 63 EUROPIUM	Gd 64 GADOLINIUM	Tb 65 TERBIUM	Dy 66 DYSPROSIUM	Ho 67 HOLMIUM	Er 68 ERBIUM	Tm 69 THULIUM	Yb 70 YTTERBIUM	Lu 71 LUTETIUM
Am 95 AMERICIUM	96 Cm CURIUM	97 Bk BERKELIUM	98 Cf CALIFORNIUM	99 Es EINSTEINIUM	100 Fm FERMIUM	101 Md MENDELEVIUM	102 No NOBELIUM	103 Lr LAWRENCIUM

Fiery &

me

* Which elements explode when mixed with water?
* Why does an airship float?
* What gives fireworks their spectacular colours?

fizzing

tals

Fiery & fizzing metals

Hydrogen sits right at the top of the periodic table. It has the simplest atoms of all, consisting of a single electron orbiting a single proton. With the two groups of light, reactive metals, hydrogen – a highly explosive gas – ensures that things begin with a bang!

Alkali metals (shown in red)

Alkaline earth metals (pink)

1	2
1 H HYDROGEN	
3 Li LITHIUM	4 Be BERYLLIUM
11 Na SODIUM	12 Mg MAGNESIUM
19 K POTASSIUM	20 Ca CALCIUM
37 Rb RUBIDIUM	38 Sr STRONTIUM
55 Cs CAESIUM	56 Ba BARIUM
87 Fr FRANCIUM	88 Ra RADIUM

Hotheaded elements

The alkali metals of Group 1 include caesium and francium, the most reactive of all the metal elements. The Group 1 metals form compounds easily and react aggressively with water. The alkaline earth metals of Group 2 are also reactive, but less so than the alkali metals. Although hydrogen is a gas, it, too, has a fiery personality and burns readily.

An average human body weighing 70 kg (154 lb) contains

7 kg (15.4 lbs) **hydrogen**

1 kg (2.2 lbs) **calcium**

140 g (5 oz) **potassium**

100 g (3.5 oz) **sodium**

35 g (1.2 oz) **magnesium**

Sodium and water

This experiment shows what happens when sodium, a Group 1 alkali metal, comes into contact with water. It was performed under laboratory conditions.

WARNING! DON'T TRY THIS AT HOME

1 A piece of sodium is placed on filter paper in a water bath. You only need a small lump . . .

2 . . . because as soon as the water soaks through the filter paper, the reaction begins!

3 *The reaction is violent. Hydrogen gas is released from the water and ignites due to the heat of the reaction.*

Alkali metals [The wildest

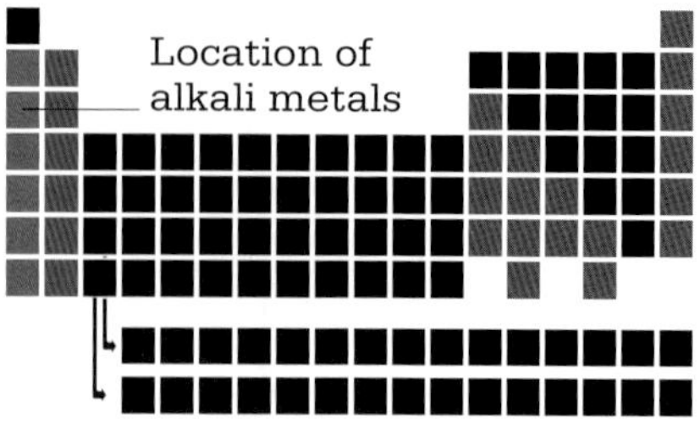

PERIODIC TABLE

The highly reactive Group 1 elements all react vigorously with water. They never occur naturally by themselves, and they form stable compounds called salts with non-metals. The alkali metals are lightweight and soft enough to cut with a knife.

3 **Li** LITHIUM

Lithium

This is the lightest of all the metals. It is often combined with other metals to form lightweight alloys for making aircraft and rocket parts. Lithium is also used in some types of battery.

What it is	A silvery-white metal
Melting point	180.54°C (356.97°F)
Boiling point	1,342°C (2,448°F)

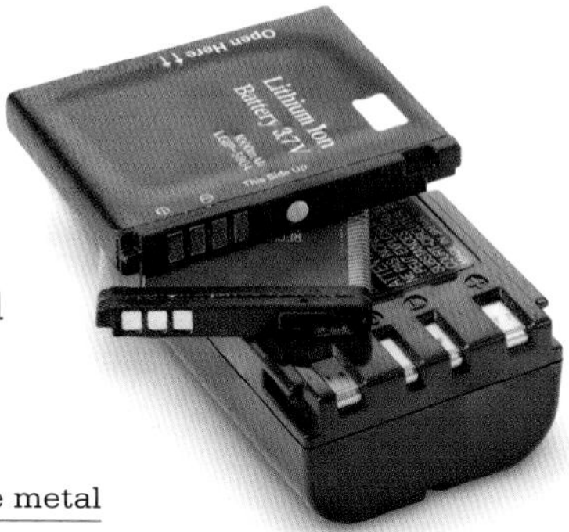
MOBILE PHONE LITHIUM–ION BATTERIES

11 **Na** SODIUM

Sodium

We eat sodium in the form of table salt, or sodium chloride (a compound of sodium and chlorine). Sodium is essential to the human body, because it helps transmit nerve signals.

What it is	A silvery-grey metal
Melting point	97.72°C (207.9°F)
Boiling point	883°C (1,621°F)

HALITE (ROCK SALT)

GPS SCREEN IN CAR

37 **Rb** RUBIDIUM

Rubidium

This element is barely solid at normal room temperature. Rubidium is used in the devices that control TVs, mobile phones, and "satnav" (satellite navigation) signals.

What it is	A grey-white metal
Melting point	39.31°C (102.76°F)
Boiling point	688°C (1,270°F)

33.7% – the salt content of the Dead Sea

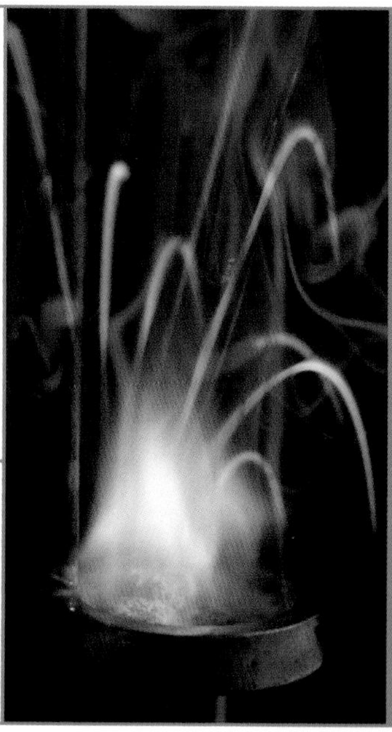

Water test

The first three alkali metals are light enough to float in water. Lithium fizzes and spits. Tiny pieces of sodium scoot over the water's surface, and larger chunks produce flames. Potassium causes an explosion. The reaction with water gets more violent as you move down Group 1.

KA-BOOM! POTASSIUM REACTING WITH WATER

87 **Fr** FRANCIUM

Francium

This metal doesn't hang around; it has a half-life of 22 minutes. In the time it takes to cook a pizza, half of its atoms decay, sending out nuclear radiation (see pp.64–65).

What it is	A radioactive metal
Predicted melting point	27°C (80°F)
Predicted boiling point	677°C (1,250°F)

URANITE (A MINERAL CONTAINING FRANCIUM)

55 **Cs** CAESIUM

Caesium

This gold-tinged element is the most reactive metal, and it also has the largest atoms. It is found in super-accurate atomic clocks. These keep time by detecting regular changes in caesium atoms.

What it is	A soft, silvery-gold metal
Melting point	28.44°C (83.19°F)
Boiling point	671°C (1,240°F)

Tick tock, atomic clock
Atomic clocks are accurate to within one second for a million years!

bunch]

CRYSTALS OF POTASSIUM DICHROMATE (A COMPOUND OF POTASSIUM, CHROMIUM, AND OXYGEN)

Potassium

19
K
POTASSIUM

Even more reactive than sodium, potassium burns with a lilac flame. Like sodium, it helps send nerve signals in the body – so eat lots of potassium-rich foods, such as bananas!

What it is	A silvery-grey metal
Melting point	63.38°C (146.08°F)
Boiling point	759°C (1,398°F)
Special features	Explodes on contact with water

More here

salt Humphry Davy
GPS atomic clock
radioactivity
nerve signals **flame tests**

Get experimenting!
Saltwater is denser than freshwater. You can test this yourself. Gently lower an egg into a glass half-full of tapwater and watch what happens. Next, stir 6–10 tablespoons of salt into the water until it dissolves. Then put the egg in the water again. What happens now?

alloy: a metallic mixture made of two or more metal elements.

half-life: the time it takes for half the atoms in a sample of a radioactive element to decay.

radioactive decay: the natural break-up of atomic nuclei in radioactive elements.

Hydrogen [The chart topper]

Element Profile

Name	Hydrogen
Symbol	H
Atomic number	1
What it is	A colourless, odourless gas
Melting point	−259.14°C (−434.45°F)
Boiling point	−252.87°C (−423.17°F)
Special features	14 times lighter than air; explosive

1
H
HYDROGEN

Hydrogen is number one in so many ways! This colourless gas has the atomic number 1 (see page 22), and it starts off the periodic table. Hydrogen was the first element to exist, and it is the lightest and most common of all the elements.

Solar flare
A solar flare is an explosion on the Sun's surface that blasts a streamer of super-hot hydrogen into space.

The Sun burns 620 million tonnes of hydrogen every second

Fuel of the stars

The element that fuels stars such as our Sun is hydrogen. Inside the Sun's core, hydrogen atoms combine to form helium atoms in a process called nuclear fusion (see pages 20–21). This process gives off energy that travels through space to heat and light our world.

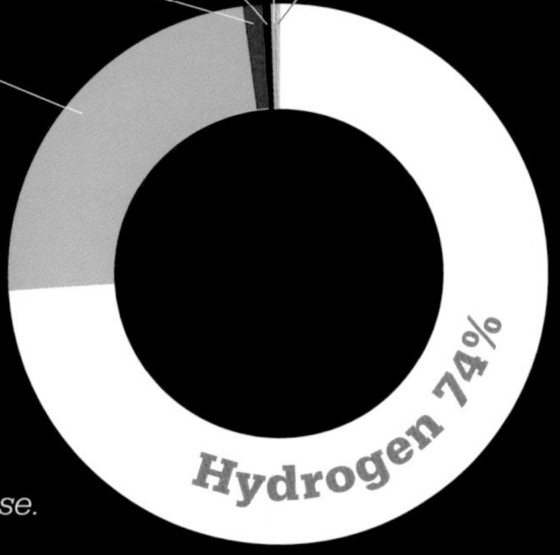
Neon 0.13%
Carbon 0.46%
Everything else 0.37%
Oxygen 1.04%
Helium 24%
Hydrogen 74%

Composition of the Universe
Hydrogen is the most common element in the Universe. Second place goes to helium. Together, the other 112 elements make up just two per cent of the matter in the Universe.

Hydrogen giants
Some giant planets are made mostly of hydrogen. Saturn's solid core is wrapped in layers of solid and liquid hydrogen, and 93 per cent of its atmosphere is hydrogen gas.

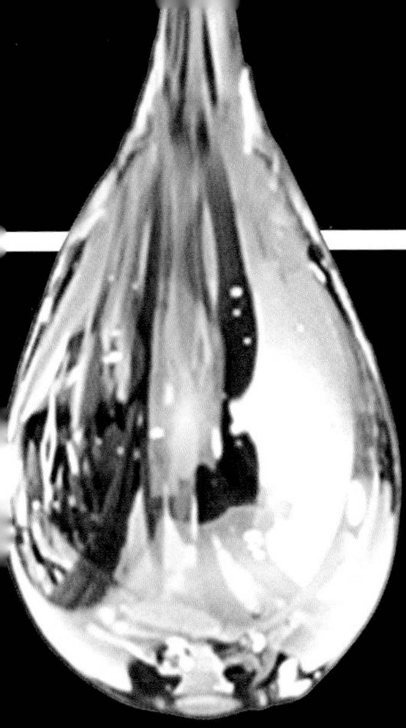

Water

There is almost no hydrogen gas on Earth, because it is so light that it rises through the atmosphere and escapes into space. But hydrogen combined with oxygen, as the compound water, covers 71 per cent of the planet's surface.

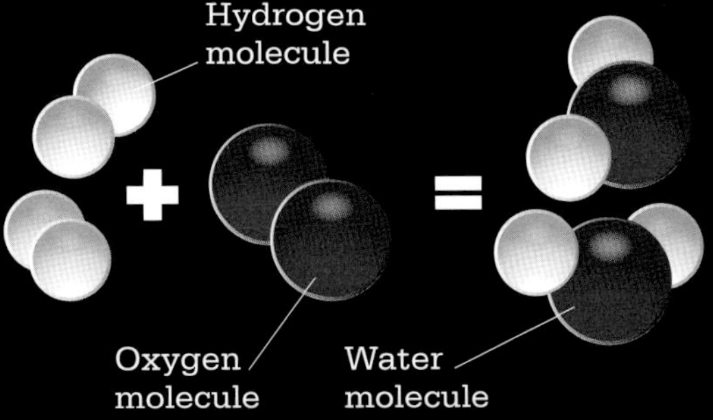
Hydrogen molecule
Oxygen molecule
Water molecule

What's in water?
Each water molecule is made of one oxygen (O) atom joined to two hydrogen (H) atoms. So scientifically water is written as "H_2O".

Producing hydrogen

Solar-power towers (right) use the Sun's energy to split water molecules and release hydrogen. It takes searing temperatures of 1,200°C (2,192°F) to achieve this.

Hydrosol-II, Spain

Solar tower
Mirrors focus sunlight onto a central tower to generate intense heat.

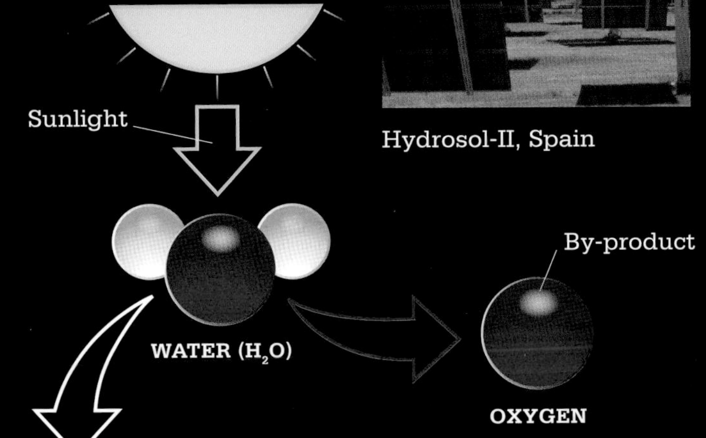
Sunlight
WATER (H_2O)
By-product
OXYGEN

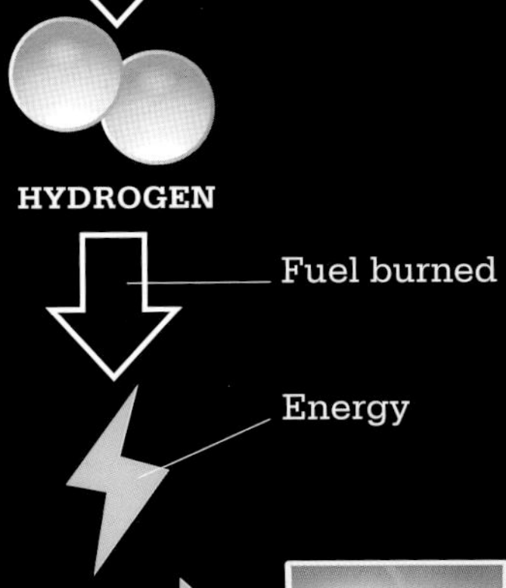
HYDROGEN
Fuel burned
Energy

Power from hydrogen
When hydrogen burns, it releases lots of energy. This energy can be used to power vehicles, or it can be converted into electricity. Hydrogen is a good alternative to using up Earth's oil supplies, and it doesn't cause pollution.

95%
of hydrogen on Earth is in the form of water

Hindenburg explodes!

Hydrogen is 14 times lighter than air, so things filled with hydrogen will fly. In the 1930s, hydrogen was used inside airships such as the *Hindenburg*, which carried passengers between Europe and the United States. But on 6 May 1937 disaster struck. The *Hindenburg* was docking at its mooring mast when it caught fire. The gas inside quickly demonstrated another of hydrogen's key characteristics – it is very explosive. The resulting fireball wrecked the airship and killed 36 people.

7:00PM Hindenburg *approaches Lakehurst Naval Station in New Jersey, where it is due to dock.*

7:21PM *The crew throws mooring ropes toward the mooring mast.*

7:24PM *The ground crew spots part of the airship's outer fabric fluttering, as if gas is leaking out.*

7:25PM Hindenburg *catches fire and the hydrogen inside quickly ignites.*

The rear of the airship explodes in a gigantic fireball and crashes to the ground.

A burst of flames shoots out of the nose, killing nine of the crew.

The exploding hydrogen gas shoots upwards because it is lighter than air, so, amazingly, many passengers travelling in the gondola under the airship survive.

The front of the airship crashes.

7:27PM *The hydrogen burns up in just 90 seconds.* Hindenburg *is reduced to twisted wreckage in 34 seconds. The diesel fuel for the airship's propellers blazes for hours.*

"It burst into flames, and it's falling, it's crashing! It's crashing terrible! Oh, my, get out of the way, please! . . . Oh, the humanity!"—HERBERT MORRISON, RADIO REPORTER

Alkaline earth metals [The

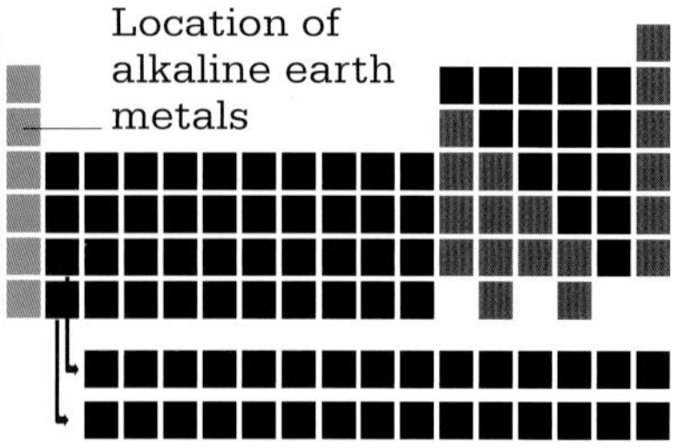
Location of alkaline earth metals
PERIODIC TABLE

The metals in this group are exceptionally light, yet strong, too, which is why they are often added to alloys. Although not as reactive as the alkali metals (see pages 30–31), they combine easily with oxygen, forming minerals that are found in Earth's crust.

12 **Mg** MAGNESIUM

Magnesium

Superlight magnesium alloys are used to reduce weight in the engines of racing cars, fast jets, and rockets. Magnesium burns with a brilliant white flame. Once alight, it is nearly impossible to extinguish.

What it is	A silvery-white metal
Melting point	650°C (1,202°F)
Boiling point	1,090°C (1,994°F)

Magnesium crystals
Magnesium can be extracted from many minerals, and also from seawater.

38 **Sr** STRONTIUM

Strontium

When exposed to the air, this silvery metal reacts with oxygen and quickly turns yellowish. Strontium burns with a bright red flame, and it is often used in fireworks.

Mayday!
The red flare of burning strontium is an internationally recognized distress signal.

What it is	A soft, silvery metal
Melting point	777°C (1,431°F)
Boiling point	1,382°C (2,520°F)

88 **Ra** RADIUM

Radium

Radioactive radium was once used to make luminous paint for instrument dials and watch hands. It was thought to be good for health and was even added to water and toothpaste – until people began dying of radiation-related illnesses.

What it is	A white, radioactive metal
Melting point	700°C (1,292°F)
Boiling point	1,737°C (3,159°F)

Autunite
Radium occurs in tiny amounts in ores such as autunite and uraninite.

5th most common element in the oceans – magnesium

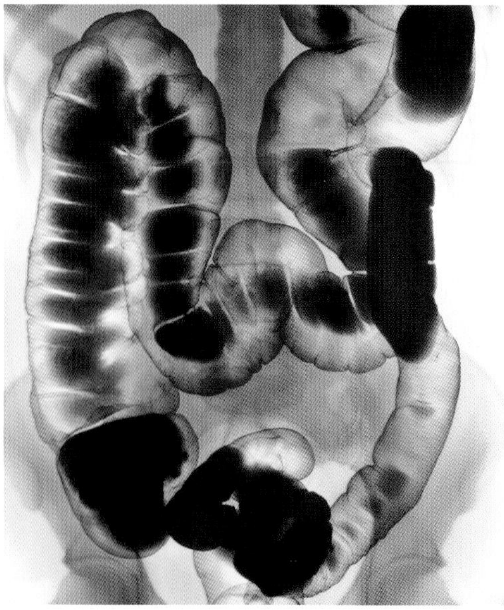

56 **Ba** BARIUM

Barium

The compound barium sulfate – barium combined with sulfur and oxygen – is given to people with stomach disorders as a "barium meal". Once swallowed, the barium shows up on X-ray photographs, allowing doctors to see what's going on in the patient's digestive system.

What it is	A silvery-grey metal
Melting point	727°C (1,341°F)
Boiling point	1,870°C (3,398°F)

Here's looking at you!
A barium meal is used to look at your guts. The heavy barium blocks the path of X-rays, showing up as dark areas in this image.

7 tonnes of ore is needed to produce just 1 g (0.035 oz) of radium

Other alkaline earth metals: Calcium (Ca)

Beryllium

4 **Be** BERYLLIUM

Tools made from beryllium-copper alloys are hard and do not create sparks when they strike a surface. They are used in places where preventing fire is crucial, such as in oil refineries.

What it is	A silvery-white metal
Melting point	1,287°C (2,349°F)
Boiling point	2,469°C (4,476°F)
Special features	Hard enough to scratch glass; among the most toxic elements

Green gems
The mineral beryl is one of the beryllium ores – the other is bertrandite. Crystals of green beryl are used to make gemstones known as emeralds.

Pure beryl is colourless. The green of emeralds is usually the result of chromium impurities.

Calcium [The builder]

20
Ca
CALCIUM

Calcium is a shiny metal, but it is seldom seen in this form because it easily joins with other elements. It is an element that builds, and its strong compounds make great construction materials – for people as well as for buildings!

Element profile

Name	Calcium
Symbol	Ca
Atomic number	20
What it is	A soft, shiny metal
Melting point	842°C (1,548°F)
Boiling point	1,484°C (2,703°F)
Special features	Very reactive; forms compounds readily; dissolves in water

Hard shells

Some sea creatures take dissolved calcium from the water and use it to make protective shells. The shells remain long after the animal dies. Some shells turn into fossils.

Stunning shells
Seashells come in a variety of shapes and sizes, often with amazing patterns and colours.

Miracle mineral

When a bone breaks, a blood clot forms at the site, and stringy fibres grow to link the broken ends. Bone-building cells called osteoblasts lay down layers of calcium minerals, from which new bone begins to form.

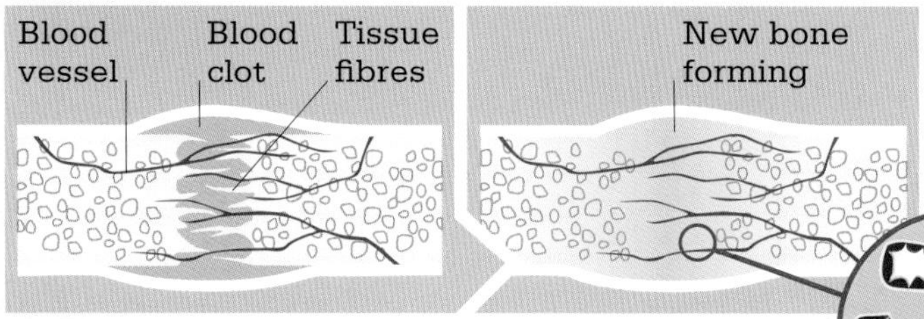
Blood vessel
Blood clot
Tissue fibres
New bone forming

Bridging the gap
New blood vessels and tissue fibres grow across the break in the bone.

Fixing the break
Osteoblasts deposit calcium minerals, which turn into bone.

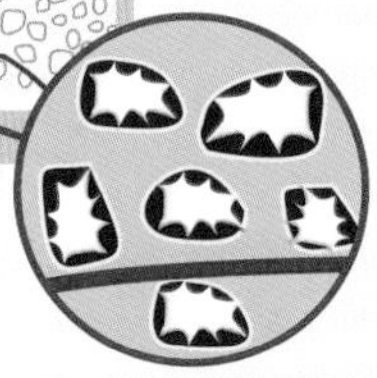

OSTEOBLASTS

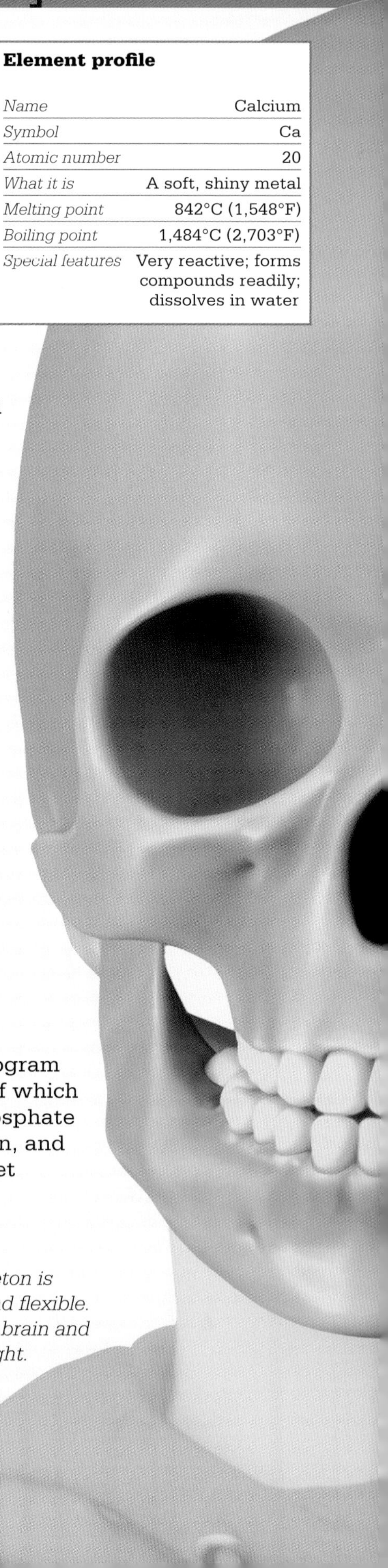

Bone health

Your body contains about 1 kilogram (2.2 pounds) of calcium, most of which is in your bones as calcium phosphate (a compound of calcium, oxygen, and phosphorus). A calcium-rich diet helps maintain healthy bones.

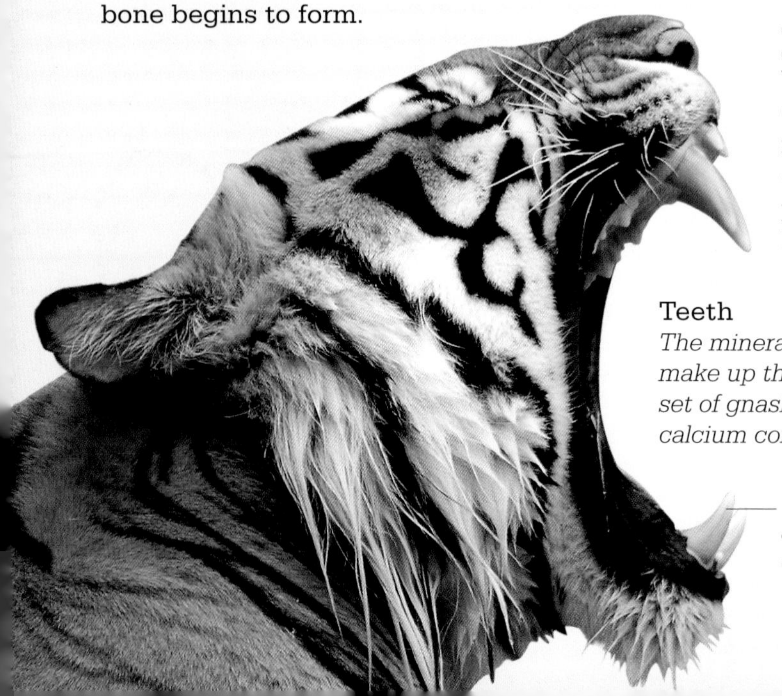

Teeth
The minerals that make up this fearsome set of gnashers are calcium compounds.

Bones
Your bony skeleton is light, strong, and flexible. It encases your brain and keeps you upright.

Teeth are protected by a hard, calcium-based coating called enamel.

Construction king

Limestone is a form of calcium carbonate (calcium combined with carbon and oxygen). Solid yet relatively easy to cut, it has been used for building since ancient times. Today, limestone is an ingredient in concrete.

Ancient pyramids
Made of limestone slabs, Egypt's pyramids were faced with blocks polished to a brilliant white shine.

Concrete giant
The Pentagon was built with 333,000 cubic metres (435,000 cubic yards) of steel-reinforced concrete.

Calcium in space

Calcium is made inside stars (see pages 20–21). When a star explodes as a supernova, it scatters the calcium into space.

X-RAY PHOTO SHOWING ONLY THE CALCIUM IN CASSIOPEIA A

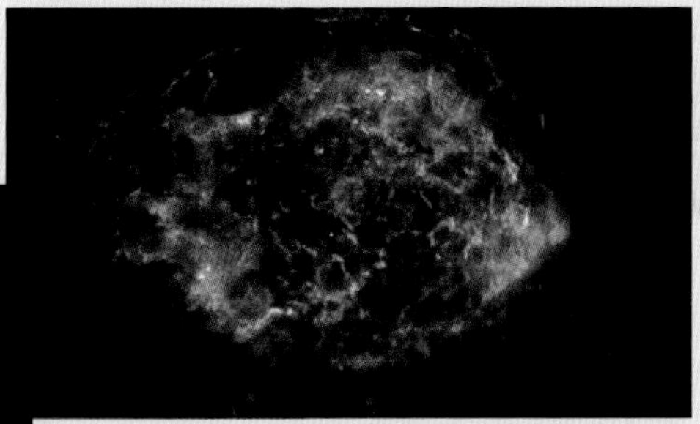

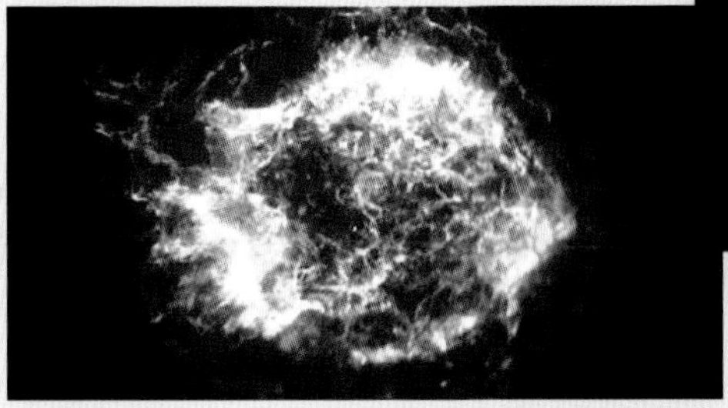

X-RAY PHOTO OF CASSIOPEIA A

Cassiopeia A
The amount of calcium in Cassiopeia A, the remains of a dead star, is equal to 1,100 times the mass of Earth.

Each year enough concrete is made to fill

400,000

Olympic swimming pools

Firework colours

This fireworks display over Washington, D.C., gets its bright colours from a range of alkali and transition metal compounds that are added to the explosive mixture. Strontium and lithium produce vivid reds as they burn, barium compounds make green, and copper creates blue. Yellow comes from sodium, while white flashes are made using aluminium, magnesium, titanium, and zirconium powders.

Mains

met

* What is Earth made of?
* How are astronauts shielded from the Sun?
* Which paint used by artists was a rat killer?

tream
tals

Mainstream metals

These shiny substances make up the vast majority of elements in the periodic table. The transition metals are generally malleable (able to be shaped without breaking), can be mixed to make alloys, and will conduct electricity. They are also the best conductors of heat – that's why they are cold to the touch, since they take heat away from your hand. Many metals are magnetic.

WARNING! DON'T TRY THIS AT HOME

Aluminium and iron oxide

In this chemical reaction, carried out under strict laboratory conditions, the poor metal aluminium frees the transition metal iron from iron oxide (a compound of iron and oxygen).

1 *Powdered iron oxide and aluminium are mixed in a glass beaker. As a precaution, the beaker is placed in a cast-iron vessel filled with sand. It's a dangerous combination!*

Types of metal

Transition metals form the main body of the periodic table. They are strong and hard, with high melting points. The poor metals, to the right, have lower melting points and are softer. The lanthanoids are all very similar and are usually set apart from the main block of metals. The same is true of the actinoids. Metalloids have both metallic and non-metallic properties.

Transition metals (shown in yellow)

Metalloids (purple)

Poor metals (blue)

Lanthanoids (green)

Actinoids (light green)

3	4	5	6	7	8	9	10	11	12	13	14	15	16
										5 B BORON			
										13 Al ALUMINIUM	14 Si SILICON		
21 Sc SCANDIUM	22 Ti TITANIUM	23 V VANADIUM	24 Cr CHROMIUM	25 Mn MANGANESE	26 Fe IRON	27 Co COBALT	28 Ni NICKEL	29 Cu COPPER	30 Zn ZINC	31 Ga GALLIUM	32 Ge GERMANIUM	33 As ARSENIC	
39 Y YTTRIUM	40 Zr ZIRCONIUM	41 Nb NIOBIUM	42 Mo MOLYBDENUM	43 Tc TECHNETIUM	44 Ru RUTHENIUM	45 Rh RHODIUM	46 Pd PALLADIUM	47 Ag SILVER	48 Cd CADMIUM	49 In INDIUM	50 Sn TIN	51 Sb ANTIMONY	52 Te TELLURIUM
57-71 La-Lu LANTHANOIDS	72 Hf HAFNIUM	73 Ta TANTALUM	74 W TUNGSTEN	75 Re RHENIUM	76 Os OSMIUM	77 Ir IRIDIUM	78 Pt PLATINUM	79 Au GOLD	80 Hg MERCURY	81 Tl THALLIUM	82 Pb LEAD	83 Bi BISMUTH	84 Po POLONIUM
89-103 Ac-Lr ACTINOIDS	104 Rf RUTHERFORDIUM	105 Db DUBNIUM	106 Sg SEABORGIUM	107 Bh BOHRIUM	108 Hs HASSIUM	109 Mt MEITNERIUM	110 Ds DARMSTADTIUM	111 Rg ROENTGENIUM	112 Cn COPERNICIUM		114 Uuq UNUNQUADIUM		116 Uuh UNUNHEXIUM

57 La LANTHANUM	58 Ce CERIUM	59 Pr PRASEODYMIUM	60 Nd NEODYMIUM	61 Pm PROMETHIUM	62 Sm SAMARIUM	63 Eu EUROPIUM	64 Gd GADOLINIUM	65 Tb TERBIUM	66 Dy DYSPROSIUM	67 Ho HOLMIUM	68 Er ERBIUM	69 Tm THULIUM	70 Yb YTTERBIUM	71 Lu LUTETIUM
89 Ac ACTINIUM	90 Th THORIUM	91 Pa PROTACTINIUM	92 U URANIUM	93 Np NEPTUNIUM	94 Pu PLUTONIUM	95 Am AMERICIUM	96 Cm CURIUM	97 Bk BERKELIUM	98 Cf CALIFORNIUM	99 Es EINSTEINIUM	100 Fm FERMIUM	101 Md MENDELEVIUM	102 No NOBELIUM	103 Lr LAWRENCIUM

3 The reaction produces molten iron, which eats right through the bottom of the beaker and even fuses the sand in the pot. Scary stuff!

2 A magnesium ribbon is lit to ignite the powdered metal mixture. As the temperature soars to 2,500°C (4,530°F), the aluminium tears the oxygen away from the iron oxide. The whole area is showered with red-hot burning metal.

Earth [What's our rocky planet

Our planet is built like an almost spherical layer cake, with tiers of different materials piled on top of one another. Amazingly, 90 per cent of Earth is made up of four elements – iron, oxygen, silicon, and magnesium!

Recipe for a planet

To make a rocky planet such as Earth, you need minerals. These substances are crystals of unreactive elements and chemical combinations of more reactive elements. Most minerals are made of a combination of oxygen and silicon.

The iron in Earth's core could make enough railroad track to circle the planet 50 billion times

Chemical copycat

The Moon seems to be chemically identical to Earth. Scientists think that it formed when a planet-size meteor collided with Earth, knocking a large chunk off into space. In 2009, NASA's LCROSS space probe crashed a spent rocket booster into the Moon and found evidence of ice in craters at its south pole.

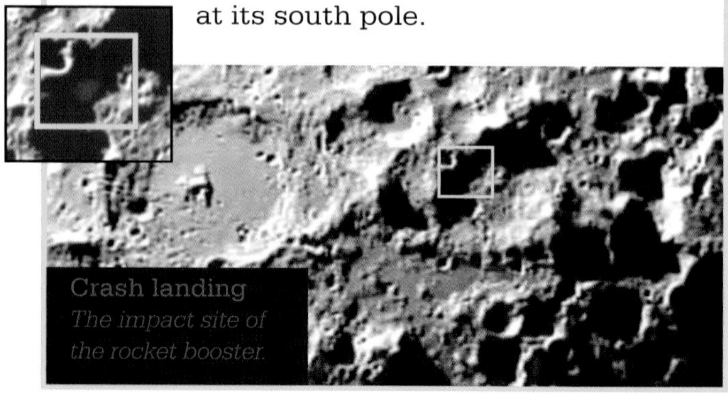

Crash landing
The impact site of the rocket booster.

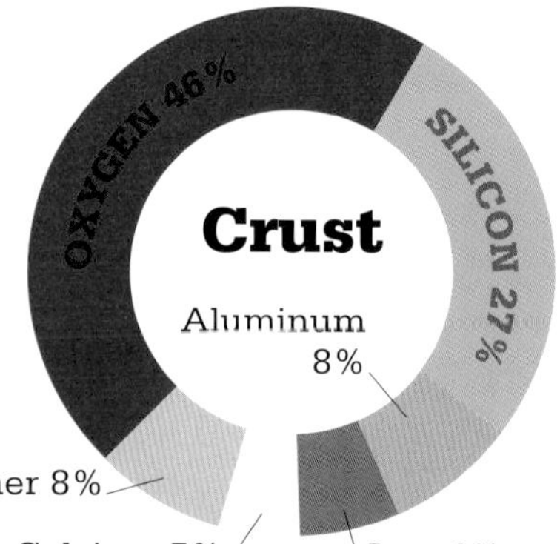

OXYGEN 46%
SILICON 27%
Crust
Aluminum 8%
Other 8%
Calcium 5%
Iron 6%

Composition of the crust
Most of the planet's oxygen is locked up in minerals in Earth's crust – the solid top layer.

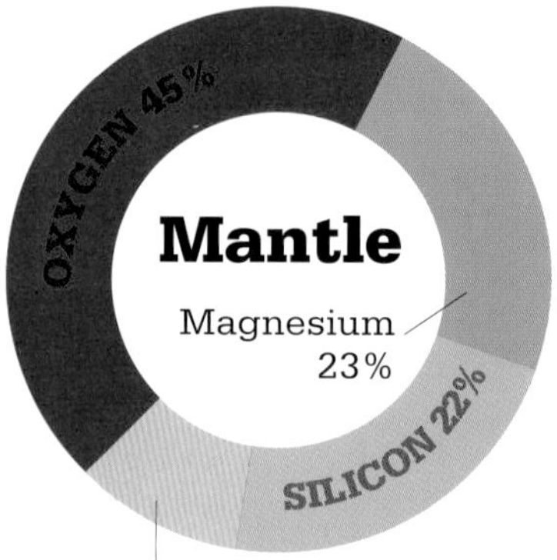

OXYGEN 45%
Mantle
Magnesium 23%
SILICON 22%
Other 10%

Composition of the mantle
The mantle makes up 70 per cent of Earth's volume. It is mainly oxygen-based compounds.

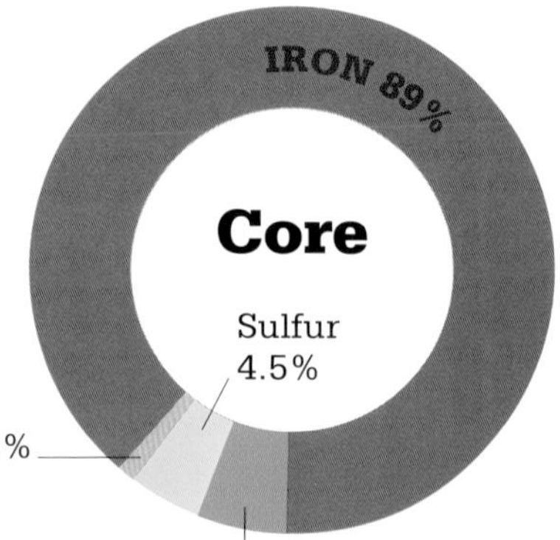

IRON 89%
Core
Sulfur 4.5%
Other 1%
Nickel 5.5%

Composition of the core
Heavy and dense elements are mostly found right in the core, or centre, of Earth.

Atmosphere
This is where all the gassy elements – mostly nitrogen and oxygen – are found.

Surface
Nearly 71 per cent of the surface is covered by water, which contains most of the hydrogen.

Crust
At 5–70 km (3–44 miles) thick, the crust is the source of all the metals and raw materials we use.

Mantle
The middle layer is 2,900 km (1,800 miles) thick and made up of oxygen, silicon, and magnesium.

Outer core
The outer core is 2,300 km (1,429 miles) thick and consists of molten iron, nickel, and sulfur.

Inner core
Earth's inner core is solid and 1,200 km (745 miles) thick. It is mostly iron and nickel.

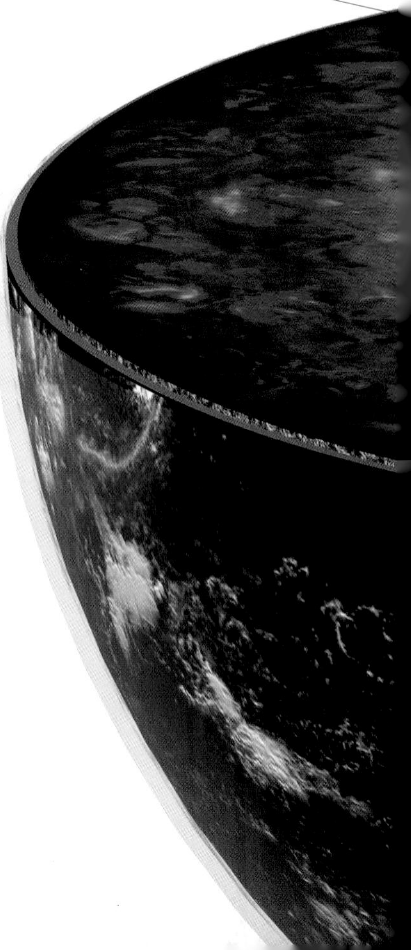

made of?]

More here

minerals crust **core** mantle **atmosphere** iron **oxygen**

Visit the Hoba Meteorite in Grootfontein, Namibia, Africa – the largest meteorite ever found and the largest known single mass of iron on Earth.

EARTH FACT FILE

Diameter:
12,755 km (7,926 miles)

Weight:
6,000 billion billion tonnes

Average distance from Sun:
150,000,000 km (93,000,000 miles)

Highest point:
Mount Everest, 8,850 m (29,035 ft)

Lowest point:
Dead Sea, 422 m (1,385 ft) below sea level

Temperature range:
–89.2°C to 57.8°C (–128.6°F to 136°F)

density: a measure of how heavy an object feels in the hand; the more weighty the atoms or the more tightly packed they are, the heavier the object feels.

mineral: a naturally occurring solid compound whose atoms are ordered in crystal patterns; many rocks are made of minerals.

A trip inside Earth

At first, Earth was a super-hot molten ball. Heavy iron and iron-loving elements – the elements that bond easily with iron – sank to the centre, because they are denser. The crust is the "scum" that floated to the surface and hardened. The atmosphere contains the lightest elements, which exist as gases.

Transition metals [Movers

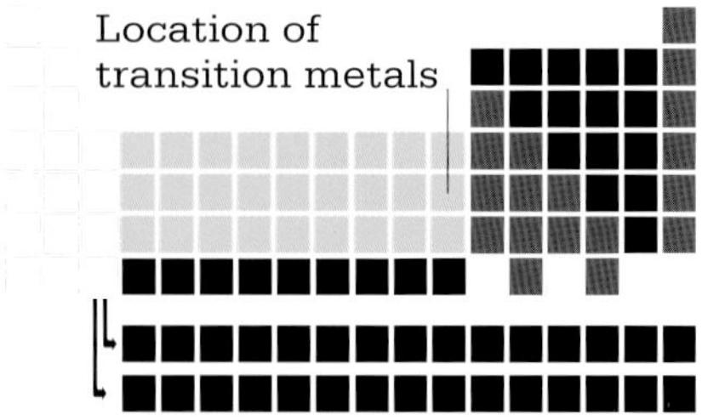

PERIODIC TABLE

Most of these metals are dense, hard, and strong, with high melting points. They conduct electricity, resist corrosion, and are easily mixed to make alloys. Transition metals also make the coloured compounds used in paint pigments and fireworks.

Guggenheim Bilbao
This Spanish museum is clad in titanium panels.

Titanium

22 **Ti** TITANIUM

Titanium is a wonder metal, incredibly strong and amazingly hard. It is used in jet engines, ships, spacecraft, sports equipment, replacement hips, dental implants, and much more.

What it is	A shiny, very tough metal
Melting point	1,668°C (3,034°F)
Boiling point	3,287°C (5,949°F)

Silver

47 **Ag** SILVER

Silver conducts electricity better than any other element, including copper (see pages 54–55). It is used for high-quality electrical wires. Germs are unable to grow on silver, so it is ideal for wound dressings and medical equipment.

Cup of champions
Silver can be polished to give a beautiful shine, which makes it popular for jewellery and trophies.

What it is	A shiny silver metal
Melting point	961.78°C (1,763.2°F)
Boiling point	2,162°C (3,924°F)

Nickel

28 **Ni** NICKEL

Super-shiny nickel does not tarnish in air. It is sometimes used to make coins. Added to alloys, it gives extra protection against rust.

What it is	A silvery, shiny, hard metal
Melting point	1,455°C (2,651°F)
Boiling point	2,913°C (5,275.4°F)

US NICKEL (5-CENT) COIN

25% – proportion of nickel in a US "nickel" coin

Other transition metals:

Vanadium (V); Chromium (Cr); Manganese (Mn); Iron (Fe); Cobalt (Co); Copper (Cu); Zinc (Zn); Zirconium (Zr); Niobium (Nb); Molybdenum (Mo); Technetium (Tc); Ruthenium (Ru); Rhodium (Rh); Cadmium (Cd); Hafnium (Hf); Tantalum (Ta); Rhenium (Re); Osmium (Os); Iridium (Ir); Platinum (Pt); Gold (Au)

Tungsten

74 **W** TUNGSTEN

Combined with carbon, tungsten forms tough tungsten carbide. This compound is used for rock drills, bulletproof armour-plating – even pen nibs!

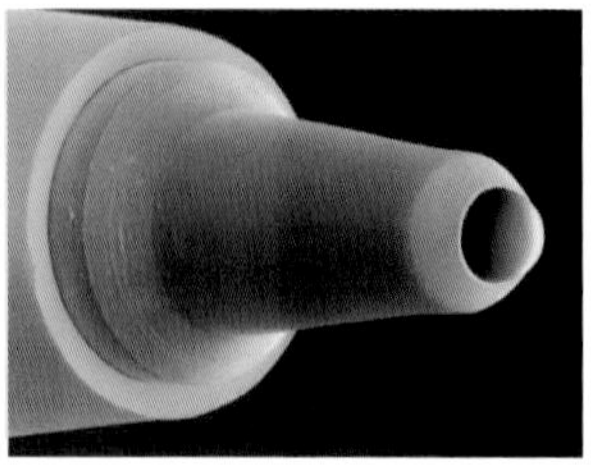

TUNGSTEN CARBIDE BALLPOINT PEN NIB

What it is	A hard, steel-grey metal
Melting point	3,422°C (6,192.6°F)
Boiling point	5,555°C (10,031°F)

Mercury

80 **Hg** MERCURY

This is the only metal that is liquid at room temperature. Mercury was used in thermometers until people realized that it is poisonous. Amalgam, a safe mercury alloy, is used in dentistry to fill cavities in teeth.

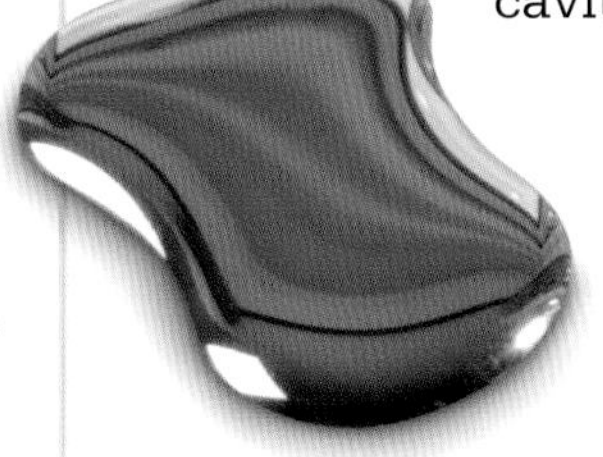

Liquid mercury
Mercury "clumps" and does not feel wet to the touch.

What it is	A slinky, silvery, liquid metal
Melting point	–38.83°C (–37.89°F)
Boiling point	356.73°C (674.11°F)

Number of years a titanium hip implant can last: 20

and shakers]

Palladium

46
Pd
PALLADIUM

This metal and its compounds are often good catalysts. Most of the palladium that is produced goes into the catalytic converters of cars (see page 17). In oil refineries, it helps split crude oil into petrol, diesel, and other useful substances (see page 89).

What it is	A shiny, silvery-white metal
Melting point	1,554.9°C (2,830.82°F)
Boiling point	2,963°C (5,365°F)
Special features	Extremely rare – and expensive

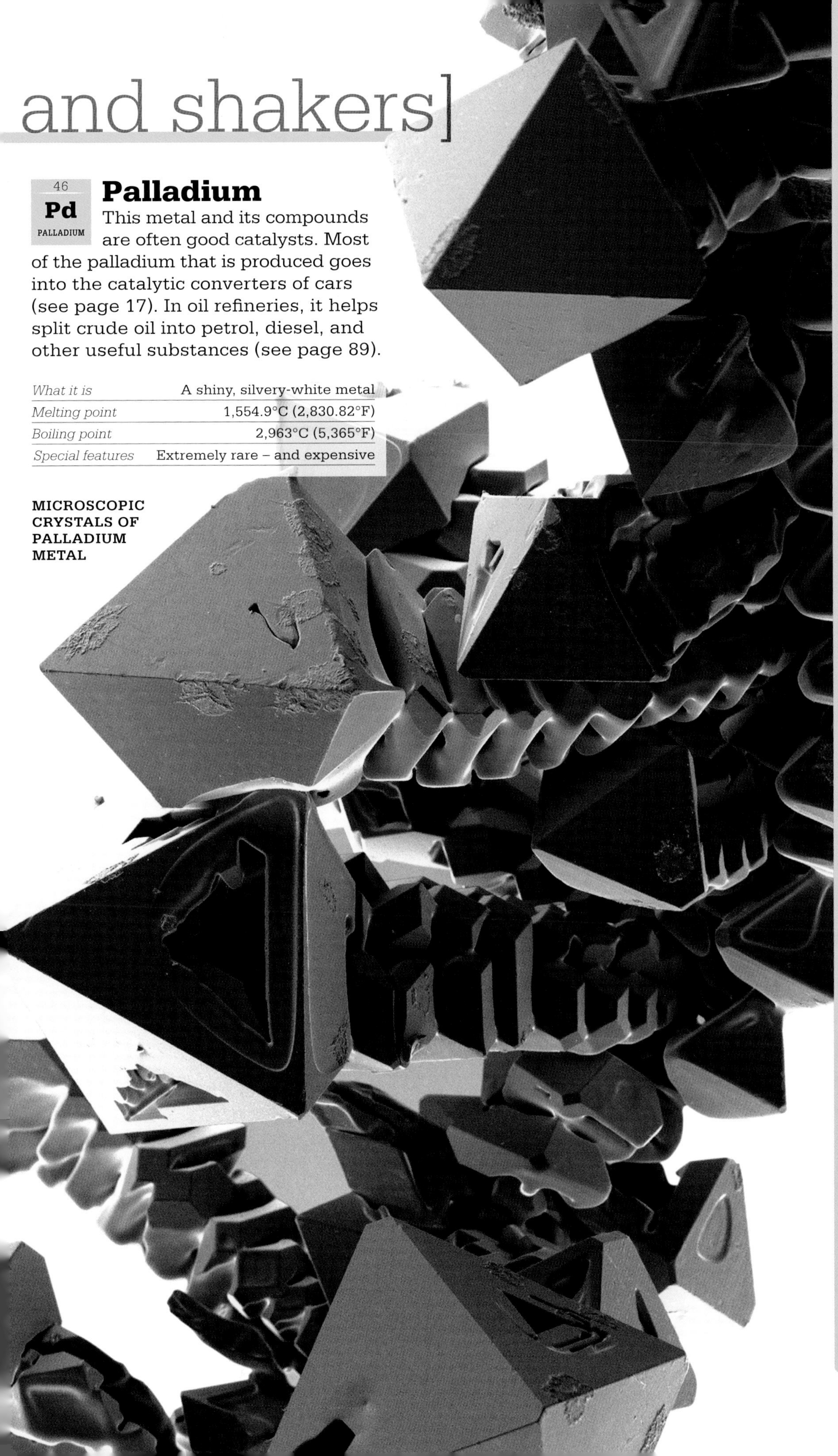

MICROSCOPIC CRYSTALS OF PALLADIUM METAL

More here

The Iron Man
by Ted Hughes

catalyst corrosion
crude oil **thermometer**
mercury barometer
pigment tungsten carbide

Visit these metal-related sites: the Chrysler Building, New York, New York; the Eiffel Tower, Paris, France; the United States Mint, Denver, Colorado

catalyst: a material that helps a chemical reaction to happen. The catalyst itself is not used up or changed in the reaction.

corrosion: the chemical breakdown of the surface of a metal.

rust: a type of corrosion that happens when iron comes into contact with oxygen and water.

Metal armour

A knight riding into battle needed to be sure that his armour was up to scratch. Its material had to be strong yet light enough to wear and flexible enough to be beaten into shape. Steel – a mixture of the hard transition metal iron and a tiny amount of carbon, a non-metal – was ideal for the task. This 17th-century steel armour, worn by the 14-year-old King Charles II of England, is decorated with layers of gold, a soft transition metal.

Gold [The king of bling]

GOLD NUGGET

79
Au
GOLD

This rare and precious metal is unchanged by air, water, or time, and it keeps its gorgeous shine forever. It is the one element that everyone throughout history has desired.

Element profile

Name	Gold
Symbol	Au
Atomic number	79
What it is	A shiny yellow metal
Melting point	1,064.18°C (1,947.52°F)
Boiling point	2,856°C (5,173°F)
Special features	The only yellow metal; soft and very unreactive

FUNERAL MASK OF TUTANKHAMEN

Everlasting value

Gold's beautiful appearance and its scarcity have always made it valuable. People have been using gold as money for thousands of years, and many countries keep gold bars in their central banks to back up their currency – gold never loses its appeal.

UNITED STATES OF AMERICA
TWENTY DOLLARS

1933 DOUBLE EAGLE, SOLD FOR $7.59 MILLION IN 2002

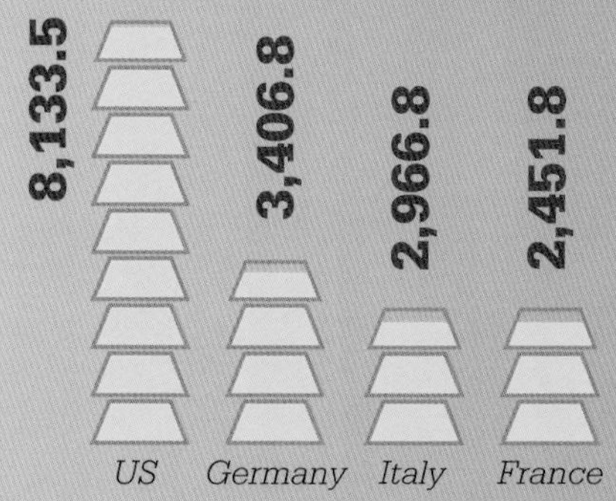

8,133.5
3,406.8
2,966.8
2,451.8
US
Germany
Italy
France

GOLD HOLDINGS (IN TONNES)

Lasting legacy

This solid gold funeral mask was made for the burial of Egyptian pharaoh Tutankhamen in 1323 BCE. Although it is more than 3,300 years old, it looks brand new!

Great gold moments

c.1323 BCE *King Tutankhamen's golden mask is created for his burial in a tomb in the Valley of the Kings, Egypt.*

ca. 950 BCE *King Solomon builds a famous temple in Jerusalem. According to the Bible, the inside is covered with pure gold.*

CAESAR

58 BCE *Julius Caesar brings back enough gold from Gaul to give 200 coins to each of his soldiers and repay all of Rome's debts.*

FABERGÉ EGG

Uses of gold

About half of all the gold in the world has been made into jewellery. Some is used for decorative objects, such as the golden Easter eggs made for Czar Alexander III by Russian jeweller Carl Gustavovich Fabergé (1846–1920).

Good conduct

Gold conducts electricity well, and, more importantly, it never rusts or tarnishes. This makes it an excellent material for contacts in electronic circuits, cable connectors, and microchips.

MICROCHIP

165,446 tonnes

–that's all the gold that has ever been mined. It would make a cube with sides just 20 m (66 ft) long.

Clear view
The astronaut is protected from glare but can still see clearly.

Precious protection
The thin coating of gold on the visor of a space helmet protects the astronaut against harmful infrared light from the Sun.

1500s *Spanish conquistadors invade the Aztec and Inca empires, seizing gold treasure and sending it back to Spain.*

1848 *The California gold rush begins at Sutter's Mill, near Sacramento. 40,000 diggers flock to California from all over the world.*

1965 *US astronaut Edward White goes on a space walk and is the first to wear a helmet with a gold-coated visor to shield him from the Sun's rays.*

Copper [Old faithful]

29
Cu
COPPER

This metal was the first to be separated from its mineral ore, about 8,000 years ago. It mixes well with other metals to form many useful alloys. Copper is a great conductor, so it is used for wires and cables in the electricity supply grid.

Element profile

Name	Copper
Symbol	Cu
Atomic number	29
What it is	A soft, malleable metal
Melting point	1,084.62°C (1,984.32°F)
Boiling point	2,927°C (5,301°F)
Special features	A superb conductor; the only reddish-orange metal

Copper reacts with the moist air over the harbour to form copper carbonate, a waterproof green coating.

Natural copper
Copper metal can occur naturally, but most copper is locked up in ores such as chalcopyrite and malachite.

The Bronze Age
By itself, copper is too soft to make long-lasting tools. About 5,000 years ago, people found that mixing copper with tin made the alloy bronze, which is much stronger.

Ancient bronze spearhead
Bronze is tough, easy to shape, and can be given a sharp edge – ideal for spears, arrows, and swords!

Blue-blooded
Spiders use copper in their blood cells to carry oxygen around their bodies. This makes their blood blue.

Tarantula spider
The redknee tarantula lives in the mountains of Mexico.

Well connected
Copper cables feed electricity from power stations to our homes. They even run under the sea, carrying currents between countries. Undersea cables also send telephone signals and link computers to the Internet.

CABLE-LAYING SHIP

Statue of Liberty
Standing at the entrance to New York Harbour is the Statue of Liberty, the world's largest copper sculpture. Copper was chosen for the statue because it is light and easy to bend, and it does not rust like iron when it comes into contact with water.

Building the statue

In 1865, French sculptor Frédéric Bartholdi was inspired to make a statue to symbolize the independence of both the French and American peoples. Work began on the 46-metre (151-foot) tall colossus in 1876.

APRIL 1876 *Lightweight copper sheets only 2.4 mm (0.1 in) thick are used to begin construction.*

SHAPING THE COPPER

MAY 1876 *The right arm is completed first and sent to New York, where it is put on display in Madison Square Park.*

1878 *The statue's head, modelled after Bartholdi's mother, is shown at the World's Fair in Paris.*

HEAD ON SHOW IN PARIS

1880 *Engineer Gustave Eiffel (who later designed the Eiffel Tower) devises an internal iron frame, to which the copper sections are attached.*

1885 *"Lady Liberty" is disassembled and shipped to the United States, but she nearly sinks during a storm en route!*

1886 *The statue is officially dedicated.*

1984 *Lady Liberty is given a makeover – her iron framework is replaced with corrosion-resistant stainless steel, and a new set of bronze doors.*

The Statue of Liberty contains 81,000 kg (179,000 lbs) of copper

Elements in art [Pigments

When the great artist Vincent van Gogh (1853–1890) worked his magic on a canvas, he used chemistry to create a riot of colour. Paints contain grains of pigment mixed with liquid. It is the elements in these pigments that produce the dazzling colours.

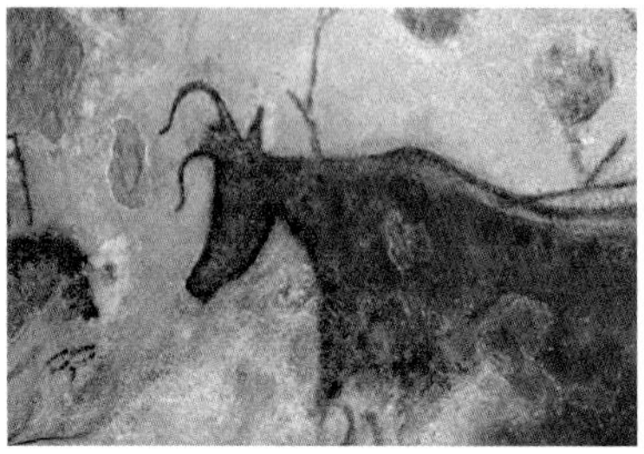

Ancient art
The paintings in the Lascaux caves of southwestern France are around 17,000 years old.

Cave art

Prehistoric artists made pictures on cave walls using natural pigments. Crushed earth (iron oxide) was used to make brown and red colours. Black came from charcoal (carbon) or the mineral stibnite (a compound of antimony and sulfur).

Elements in the paint

In van Gogh's time, paints were often named after the elements they contained, as in lead white or chrome yellow. Some of these paints were toxic. Many modern pigments contain compounds of transition metals, which produce vivid colours.

CARBON

Bone black
Charred, crushed bones were the source of the black in this paint. Today, bone black is made with ferric (iron) oxide.

LEAD

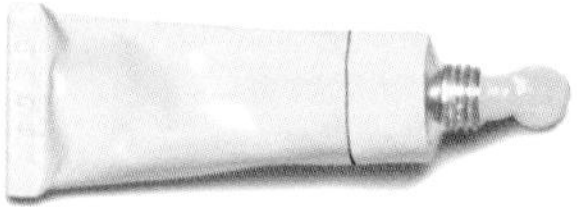

Lead white
White paints contained poisonous lead until the 1950s. They are now made with titanium dioxide or zinc oxide.

Van Gogh's Bedroom in Arles
Vincent van Gogh is famous for the vibrant colours he used in his pictures. He produced this oil painting of his bedroom in 1889.

Pigment

Solid grains of coloured chemical compounds

+

Binder

Hydrocarbons (compounds of hydrogen and carbon) that hold the paint pigments together

and colour]

Paris green paint was so toxic that it was also used as rat poison

Vermilion (red)
This colour was produced by a mercury compound extracted from the mineral cinnabar. Modern reds use compounds of cadmium.

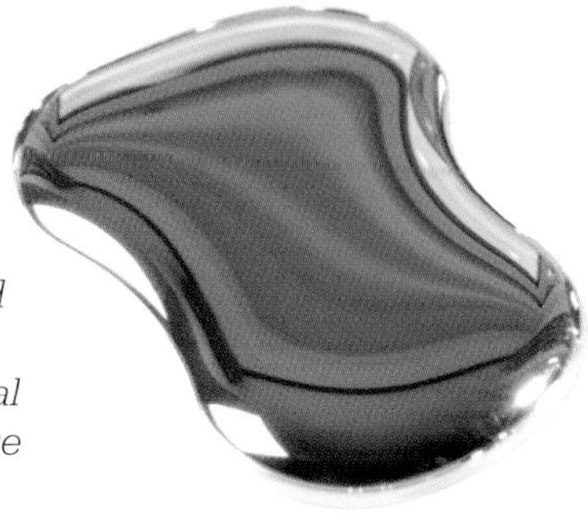

MERCURY

Prussian blue
Made of a compound of iron, this colour was also used by engineers, which is why their drawings are known as blueprints.

IRON

Cadmium yellow
The compound cadmium sulfide produces this yellow. Van Gogh used chrome yellow, made with lead and chromium.

CADMIUM

Paris green
This deep-emerald copper compound contains toxic arsenic. It may have poisoned some of the artists who used it.

COPPER

+ **Solvent**
Alcohol, oil, or water added to keep the paint liquid
=

Iron [A tough cookie]

Iron from space
Meteorites – space rocks that crash to Earth – are often extremely rich in iron.

26
Fe
IRON

Hard iron can be moulded or beaten into almost any shape, making it the most useful of all the metals. Its main drawback is that, without protection, it can rust, combining with oxygen to become flaky and weak.

Element profile

Name	Iron
Symbol	Fe
Atomic number	26
What it is	A strong metal
Melting point	1,538°C (2,800°F)
Boiling point	2,861°C (5,182°F)
Special features	Can be magnetized; forms most of Earth's core

The Iron Age

About 3,500 years ago, people learned how to separate iron from its ore by smelting (heating the ore with charcoal, coal, or coke). Iron gradually replaced bronze (see page 54) for tools and weapons.

Iron dagger (6th century BCE)
Iron is much harder than bronze, so it made superior weapons.

From iron to steel
The iron made by smelting has a high carbon content. Removing most of this carbon makes steel, which is 1,000 times stronger than iron.

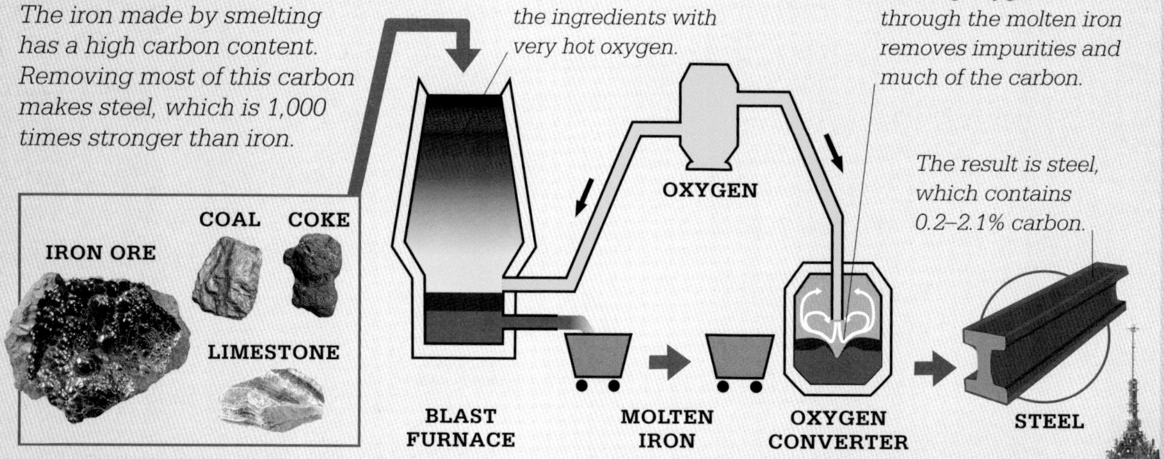
The furnace blasts the ingredients with very hot oxygen.
Blowing oxygen through the molten iron removes impurities and much of the carbon.
The result is steel, which contains 0.2–2.1% carbon.
OXYGEN
IRON ORE
COAL
COKE
LIMESTONE
BLAST FURNACE
MOLTEN IRON
OXYGEN CONVERTER
STEEL

Going up!

Iron and steel are ideal for constructing strong, stable structures such as towers, bridges, and the frames of concrete skyscrapers. These metals allow us to build ever higher and higher.

EMPIRE STATE BUILDING, NEW YORK, NEW YORK (1931)
381 m
1,250 ft

The limestone and granite cladding (outer skin) covers a steel frame weighing 55,000 tonnes.

EIFFEL TOWER, PARIS, FRANCE (1889)
324 m
1,063 ft

The tower is made of iron girders.

GOLDEN GATE BRIDGE, SAN FRANCISCO, CALIFORNIA (1937)
227.4 m
746 ft

HOME INSURANCE BUILDING, CHICAGO, ILLINOIS (1884)
42 m
138 ft

Attractive metal

Iron is used to make magnets, which attract some metals. The magnetic force is strongest at the north (N) and south (S) poles of a magnet.

Poles apart

A compass uses a metal pointer to show direction. Here you can see how a magnet's poles attract the metal pointers of compasses.

PETRONAS TOWERS, KUALA LUMPUR, MALAYSIA (1998)

452 m

1,483 ft

Together, the towers contain about (37,000 cu m (1.3 million cu ft) of steel.

TAIPEI 101, TAIPEI, TAIWAN (2004)

509 m

1,670 ft

BURJ KHALIFA, DUBAI, UNITED ARAB EMIRATES (2009)

828 m

2,717 ft

The aluminium, steel, and glass cladding of the Burj Khalifa – the world's tallest building – would cover 25 football fields!

Iron from ore

A worker in fireproof clothing heaps sand onto the red-hot slag (waste) emerging from a blast furnace. This type of furnace is used to extract iron from its rocky ore, in which the iron is bound tightly to oxygen. The temperature inside the furnace reaches a searing 2,400°C (4,352°F) as the ore is blasted by hot air and burning coke (a form of carbon). The heat causes the carbon to combine with the oxygen in the ore, allowing the iron to flow out of the rock as liquid metal.

Rare earth metals

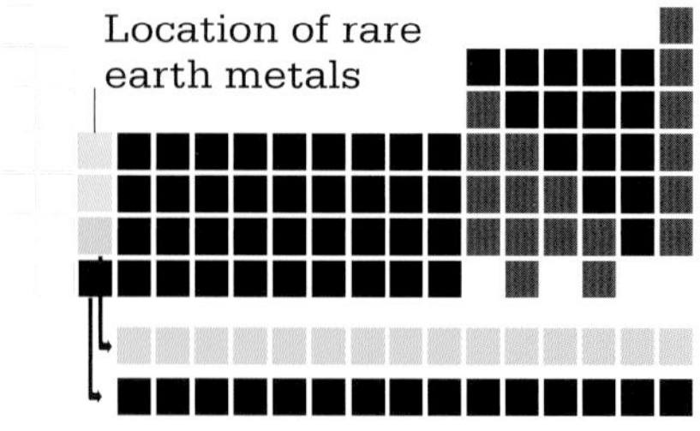

PERIODIC TABLE

The elements yttrium and scandium, along with the lanthanoids, are called rare earth metals. These soft metals are used for strong magnets and to generate laser beams. Despite their name, most are not rare, but they are difficult to extract from Earth's crust.

Yttrium

39 **Y** YTTRIUM

YAG lasers use crystals of yttrium-aluminium-garnet. These powerful lasers can cut though metal, but they are also precise enough for use in surgery.

What it is	A silvery-white transition metal
Melting point	1,526°C (2,779°F)
Boiling point	3,336°C (6,037°F)

97% of all rare earth metals are extracted in China

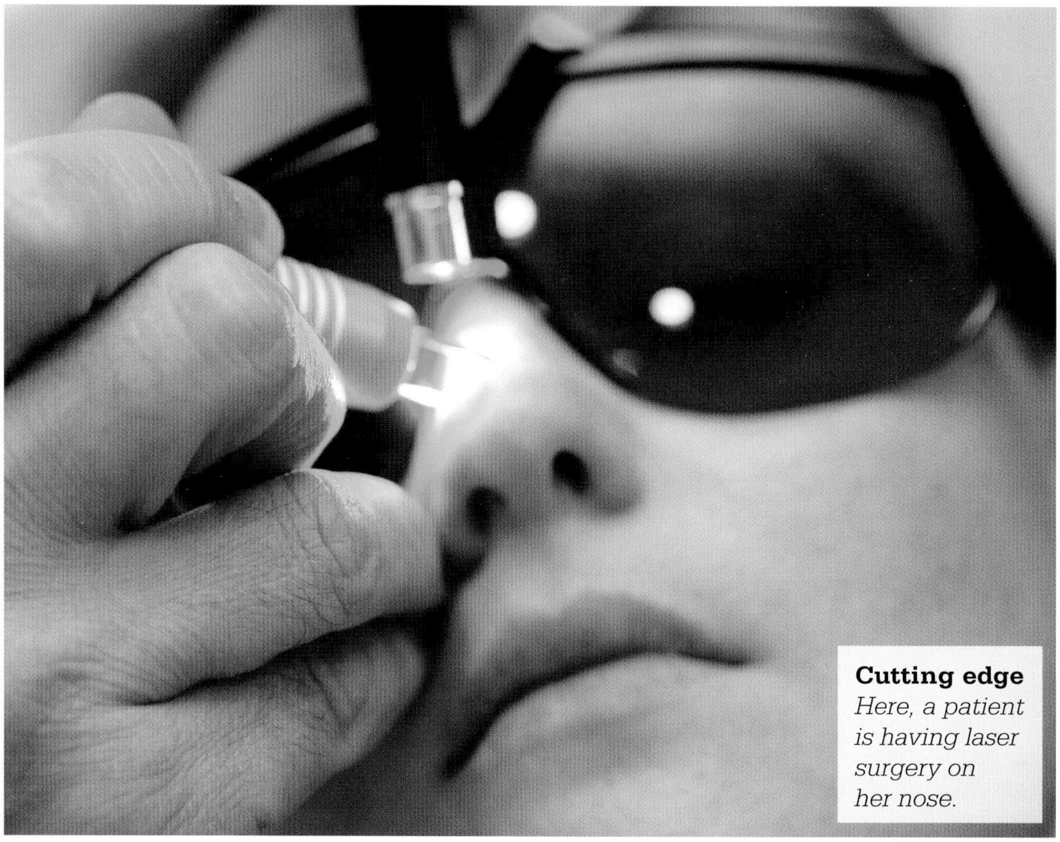

Cutting edge
Here, a patient is having laser surgery on her nose.

Turning turbines
Neodymium permanent magnets are used in the electric generators of wind turbines.

Neodymium

60 **Nd** NEODYMIUM

Neodymium magnets (made from a neodymium-iron-boron alloy) are the world's strongest permanent magnets. They are used in everything from microphones and loudspeakers to mobile phone vibrators, electric motors, and computer hard drives.

What it is	A bright, silvery, reactive metal
Melting point	1,024°C (1,875°F)
Boiling point	3,100°C (5,612°F)

Element haven

The small Swedish town of Ytterby has four elements named after it – yttrium, ytterbium, terbium, and erbium. In all, seven new elements were discovered in minerals from a local mine. The other three are gadolinium, holmium, and thulium.

PLAQUE COMMEMORATING THE ELEMENTS FOUND AT YTTERBY

Other rare earth metals:

Scandium (Sc); Lanthanum (La); Cerium (Ce); Praseodymium (Pr); Promethium (Pm); Samarium (Sm); Europium (Eu); Gadolinium (Gd); Terbium (Tb); Dysprosium (Dy); Holmium (Ho); Erbium (Er); Thulium (Tm); Ytterbium (Yb); Lutetium (Lu)

Heavy elements

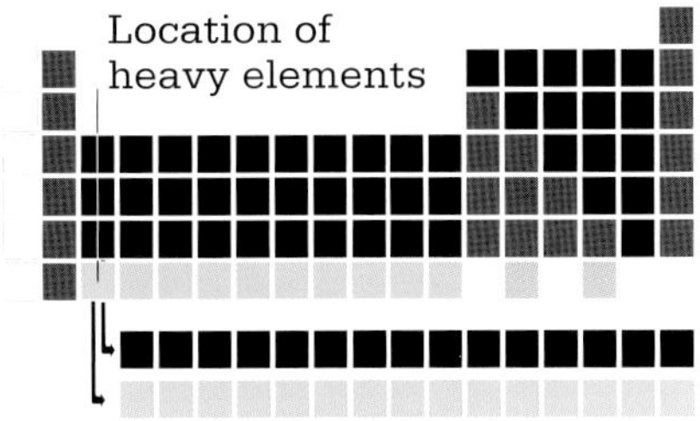
Location of
heavy elements

PERIODIC TABLE

The last part of the periodic table is home to the "heavies" – radioactive elements (see pages 64–65) with 89 or more protons in their nuclei. Those heavier than uranium, which has 92 protons, do not occur naturally on Earth but are created artificially.

Uranium

92 **U** URANIUM

The nuclei of uranium atoms can be split, releasing huge amounts of energy and causing a chain reaction in which other nuclei are split. The chain reaction may be controlled in a nuclear reactor or uncontrolled in an atomic bomb explosion.

What it is	A radioactive, silvery-grey metal
Melting point	1,132.2°C (2,070°F)
Boiling point	3,927°C (7,101°F)

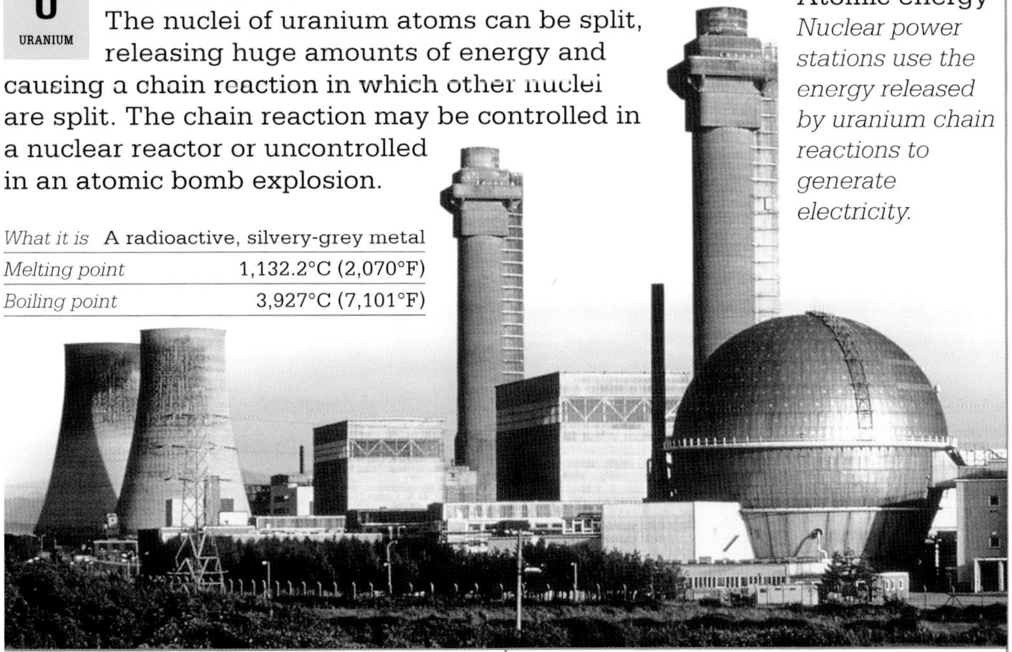

Atomic energy
Nuclear power stations use the energy released by uranium chain reactions to generate electricity.

Plutonium

94 **Pu** PLUTONIUM

This element is used to make atomic bombs, so it is closely guarded. A lump of plutonium will glow like a hot coal as it produces heat by alpha radiation (see page 65).

What it is	A reactive, silvery-grey metal
Melting point	639.4°C (1,182.9°F)
Boiling point	3,230°C (5,846°F)

Atomic explosion
The blast from an atomic bomb destroys everything within several kilometres, and throws deadly radiation up into the air.

Americium

95 **Am** AMERICIUM

This element forms a vital part of the electrical circuits of smoke detectors. Americium is the only radioactive element that you are ever likely to have in your house!

What it is	A silvery-white metal
Melting point	1,176°C (2,149°F)
Boiling point	2,607°C (4,725°F)

Einsteinium

99 **Es** EINSTEINIUM

Element 99 was named after the German-born physicist Albert Einstein. It was created in the testing of "Ivy Mike", the first hydrogen atomic bomb, which blew up the small island of Enewetak, in the Pacific Ocean.

ALBERT EINSTEIN (1879–1955)

What it is	A silvery metal
Melting point	860°C (1,580°F)
Boiling point	Unknown

Radioactive waste from nuclear power stations remains unsafe for 20,000 years

Other heavy elements:

Actinium (Ac); Thorium (Th); Protactinium (Pa); Neptunium (Np); Curium (Cm); Berkelium (Bk); Californium (Cf); Fermium (Fm); Mendelevium (Md); Nobelium (No); Lawrencium (Lr); Rutherfordium (Rf); Dubnium (Db); Seaborgium (Sg); Bohrium (Bh); Hassium (Hs); Meitnerium (Mt); Darmstadtium (Ds); Roentgenium (Rg); Copernicium (Cn); Ununquadium (Uuq); Ununhexium (Uuh)

Radioactive elements

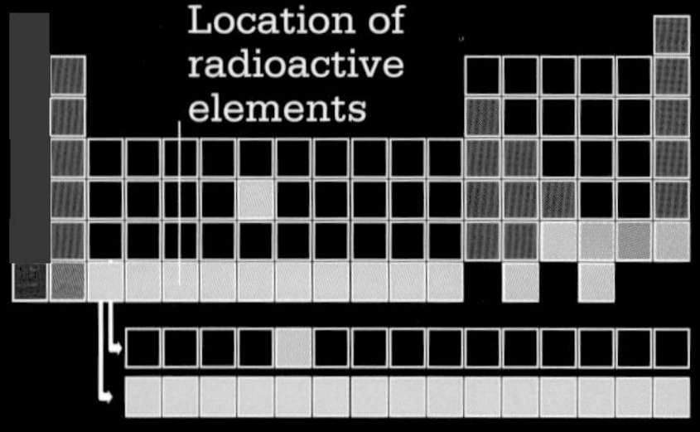
Location of radioactive elements
PERIODIC TABLE

Radioactivity is like a sickness that affects the atoms of some elements, causing their nuclei to break up. These unstable elements split apart without warning and without outside help, releasing a burst of dangerous radiation.

Atomic struggle

There is a terrific struggle going on in an atom's nucleus. Positively charged protons try to push each other apart, but a force called the strong nuclear force binds them tightly to neutrons. If the strong nuclear force breaks down, the nucleus decays (splits), sending out radiation.

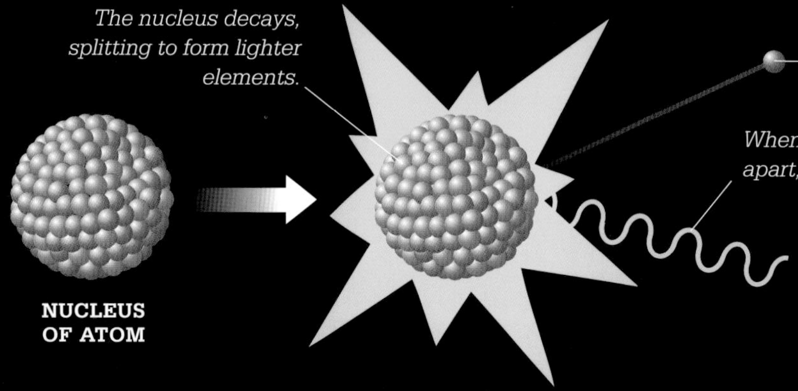
The nucleus decays, splitting to form lighter elements.
Electrically charged particles may be fired out of the nucleus.
When the nucleus breaks apart, it releases energy.
NUCLEUS OF ATOM

Nuclear decay
A nucleus can split and release radiation at any time.

1kg (2.2 lb) of uranium could power the entire USA for nearly 3 minutes

Supernova
Uranium, plutonium, and many other radioactive elements are made when a massive star explodes as a supernova.

Half-life

The time it takes for half of the atoms in a radioactive material to decay is called the half-life. Elements with a shorter half-life are more unstable and decay more quickly.

Sample half-lives
Half-lives range from the merest fraction of a second to over two trillion trillion years!

1.3 billion years
Potassium-40
(found in bananas)
2.2 trillion trillion years
Tellurium-128
(in rare minerals)
4.5 billion years
Uranium-238
(in uranium ore)

Radiation types

There are three types of radiation. Alpha particles consist of two neutrons and two protons. Beta particles are similar to electrons. Gamma rays are intense bursts of energy. Exposure to very large doses of radiation – as in a nuclear accident or explosion – can be lethal.

Slow, heavy alpha particles are stopped by a sheet of paper.

Aluminium foil stops fast, light beta particles.

It takes a thick layer of lead to stop gamma rays.

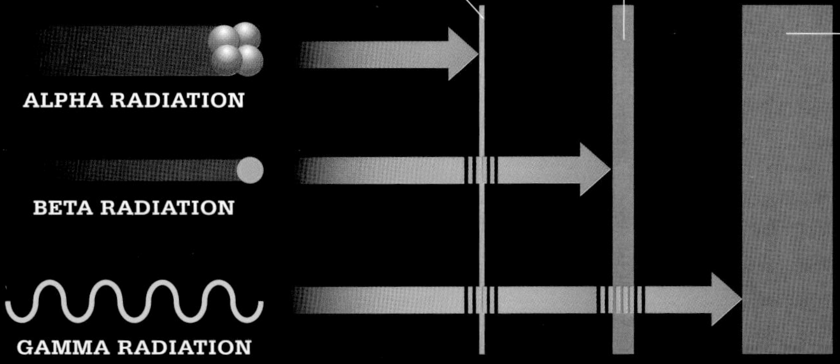
ALPHA RADIATION
BETA RADIATION
GAMMA RADIATION

Stopping radiation
Alpha particles are the easiest type of radiation to stop, but they are also the most harmful. They damage the DNA in your body's cells.

Energy from atoms

Radioactive uranium is the most energy-rich fuel. Nuclear power stations split uranium nuclei to release energy, which they then use to generate electricity.

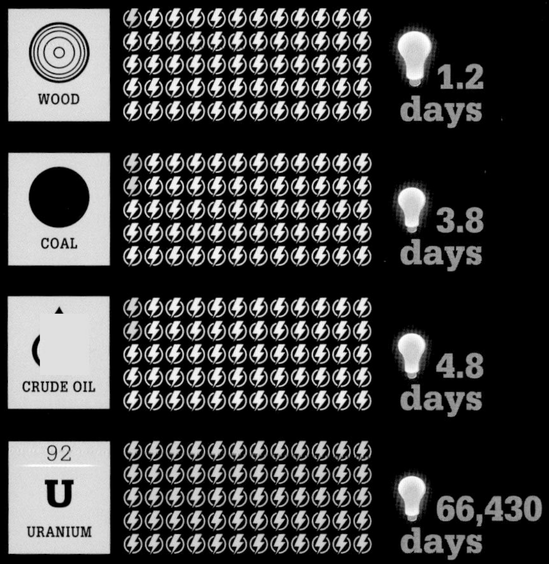
WOOD
1.2 days
COAL
3.8 days
CRUDE OIL
4.8 days
92
U
URANIUM
66,430 days

Comparing fuels
This chart shows how long 1 kg (2.2 lb) of different fuels will light a 100-watt bulb.

Background radiation

We are exposed to a small amount of natural radiation every day. This harmless dose is known as background radiation. It comes from space, rocks, soil, plants, food, and animals, as well as from artificial sources.

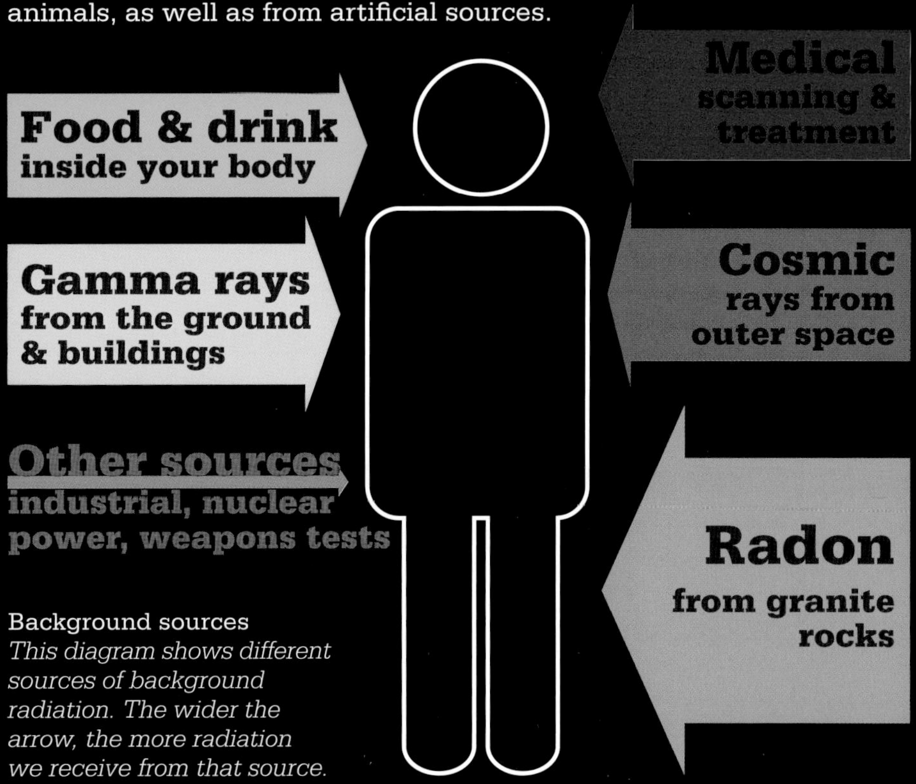
Food & drink
inside your body
Gamma rays
from the ground & buildings
Other sources
industrial, nuclear power, weapons tests
Medical
scanning & treatment
Cosmic
rays from outer space
Radon
from granite rocks

Background sources
This diagram shows different sources of background radiation. The wider the arrow, the more radiation we receive from that source.

The number after each element is the sum of protons and neutrons in its nuclei.

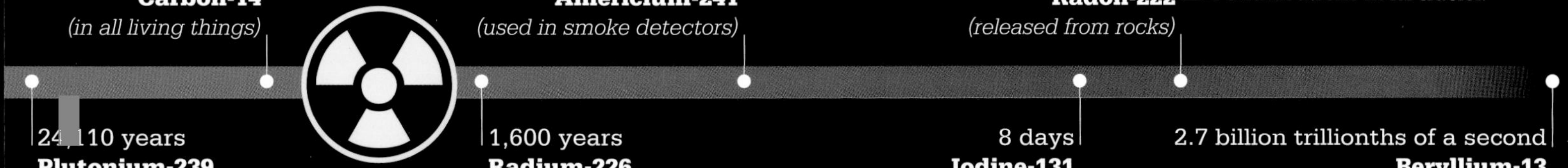
5,715 years
Carbon-14
(in all living things)
432.2 years
Americium-241
(used in smoke detectors)
3.8 days
Radon-222
(released from rocks)
24,110 years
Plutonium-239
(used in nuclear fuel and weapons)
1,600 years
Radium-226
(discovered by Marie Curie)
8 days
Iodine-131
(hazardous nuclear waste)
2.7 billion trillionths of a second
Beryllium-13
(created in stars)

Marie Curie

Polish-born Marie Curie (1867–1934) was a real superstar of science. In addition to discovering the radioactive elements polonium and radium, she won Nobel Prizes in physics (1903) and chemistry (1913) – the only person to win in multiple sciences. Marie Curie died from leukaemia at the age of 66, probably due to prolonged exposure to radioactive substances. The element curium (96 on the periodic table) is named after her.

Poor metals [Magnificent

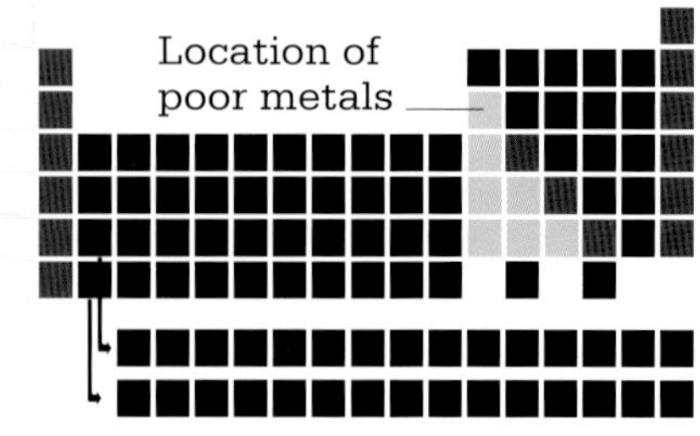

Location of poor metals

PERIODIC TABLE

These seven elements lie between the transition metals and the metalloids. They are known as "poor" metals because they are softer and have lower melting points than transition metals. They include some of the most useful elements on Earth.

31 **Ga** GALLIUM

Gallium

This strange metal melts in the hand. Combined with arsenic as gallium-arsenide, it is used in solar cells, which use sunlight to make electricity, and as a semiconductor (see page 73) in electronic circuits.

What it is	A shiny, soft metal
Melting point	29.76°C (85.57°F)
Boiling point	2,204°C (3,999°F)

A poor metal on Mars
Gallium forms part of the electronic circuits of NASA's Mars Exploration Rovers.

MOBILE PHONE TOUCH SCREEN

49 **In** INDIUM

Indium

Indium is soft enough to dent with your fingernail. One of its alloys, indium tin oxide, not only conducts electricity but is also see-through. This alloy is often used in touch-screen devices.

What it is	A soft, silvery-grey metal
Melting point	156.6°C (313.9°F)
Boiling point	2,072°C (3,762°F)

CASSERITE, A TIN OXIDE ORE MINERAL

50 **Sn** TIN

Tin

Tin has a relatively low melting point. It is an ingredient in the alloy solder, which is melted to join metal parts. This metal is good at resisting corrosion, so metal objects are sometimes given a protective coat of tin.

What it is	A soft, shiny metal
Melting point	231.93°C (449.47°F)
Boiling point	2,602°C (4,716°F)

THALLIUM

81 **Tl** THALLIUM

Thallium

Once used as a poison for rats and ants, this highly toxic metal rapidly causes the body's major organs to fail. Today, thallium compounds are used in glass-making and in electronic components.

What it is	A soft, silvery-grey metal
Melting point	304°C (579°F)
Boiling point	1,473°C (2,683°F)

8,400 years old – the age of lead beads discovered in Turkey

50 aluminium cans are made every second in the USA

13 **Al** ALUMINIUM

Aluminium

Although more expensive to produce than iron (see pages 58–59), aluminium is lighter and does not rust. It combines with oxygen to form a weatherproof coating of aluminum oxide.

What it is	A light metal, silvery-white
Melting point	660.32°C (1,220.58°F)
Boiling point	2,519°C (4,566°F)

Douglas C-53D Skytrooper
The fuselages (bodies) of aircraft are assembled from sheets of lightweight aluminium alloy.

83 **Bi** BISMUTH

Bismuth

Bismuth is used in fire sprinkler systems because it melts easily. The heat of a fire melts the metal, triggering the sprinklers. It is also used in medicines for soothing stomach ulcers.

BISMUTH CRYSTAL

What it is	A silvery-white metal
Melting point	271.3°C (520.3°F)
Boiling point	1,564°C (2,847°F)

Galena forms grey to silvery-grey crystals.

82
Pb
LEAD

Lead

Lead is a heavy metal, but it is not as dense as tungsten (see page 48) or uranium (see page 63). It was used for water pipes until people realized that dissolved lead is poisonous. Today, lead is a popular roofing material.

What it is	A shiny metal; quickly turns dull
Melting point	327.46°C (621.43°F)
Boiling point	1,749°C (3,180°F)
Special features	Soft and very easy to shape

Lead ore
Galena is the main ore of lead. It is often found near deposits of silver.

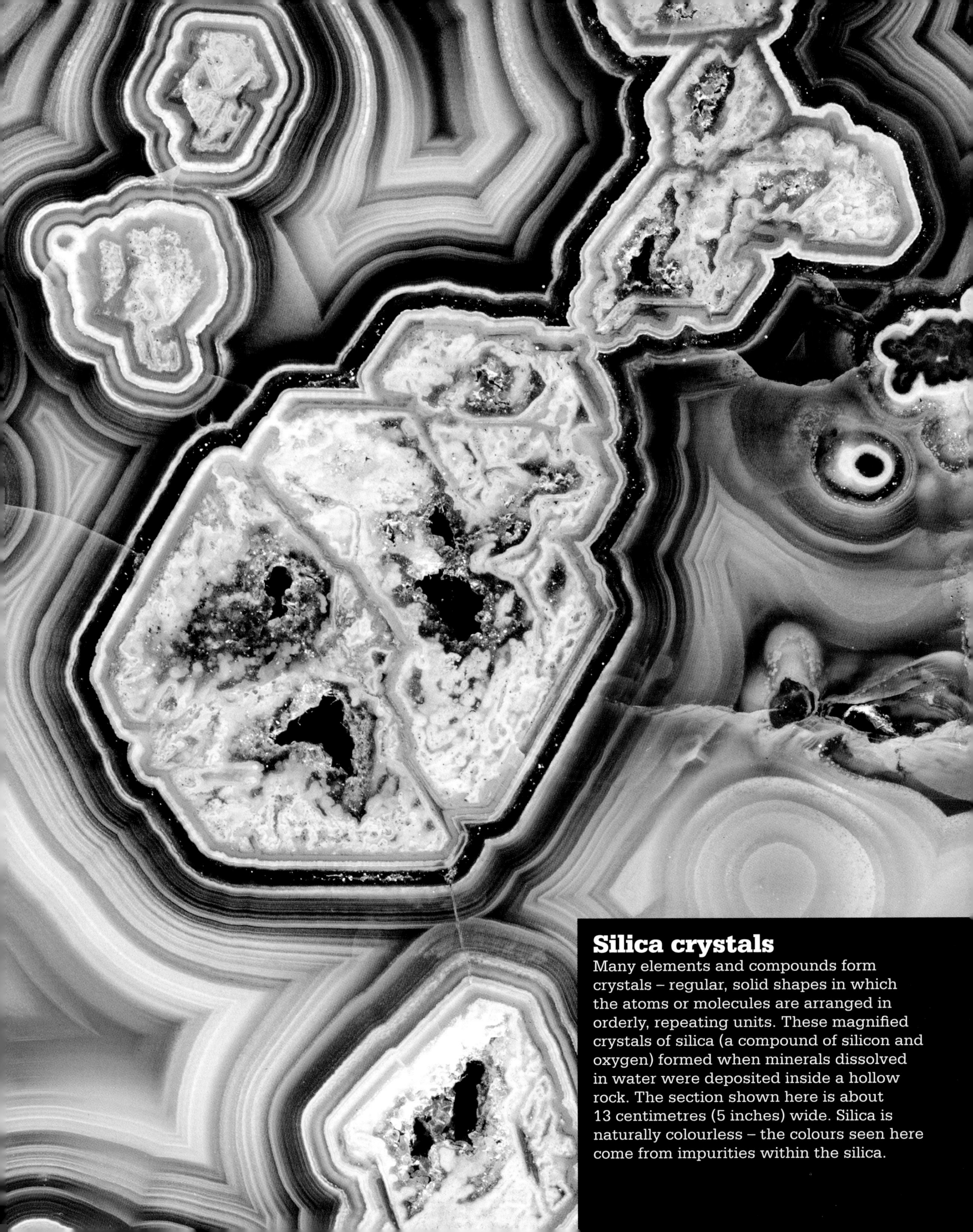

Silica crystals

Many elements and compounds form crystals – regular, solid shapes in which the atoms or molecules are arranged in orderly, repeating units. These magnified crystals of silica (a compound of silicon and oxygen) formed when minerals dissolved in water were deposited inside a hollow rock. The section shown here is about 13 centimetres (5 inches) wide. Silica is naturally colourless – the colours seen here come from impurities within the silica.

Metalloids [The changelings]

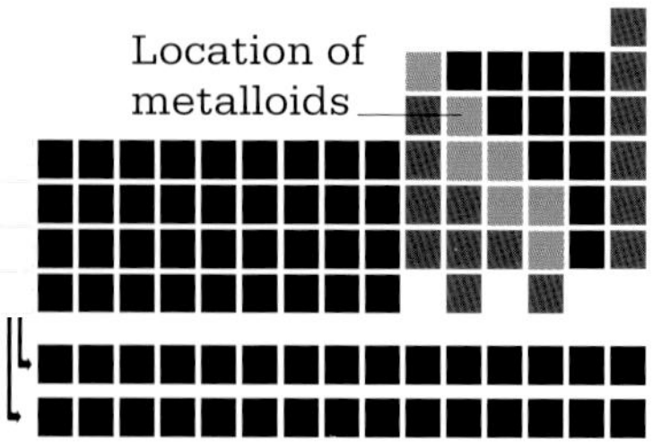

PERIODIC TABLE

A thin, diagonal line of metalloids runs across the right of the periodic table. As if undecided what they want to be, these elements have properties of both metals and non-metals. Most metalloids can occur in different forms, known as allotropes.

Allotropes

In metalloids and some other elements, the atoms can link up in more than one way to produce allotropes. These are different forms of the same element that look and behave differently.

HARD ARSENIC

SOFT ARSENIC

Hard or soft?
Arsenic occurs as both a brittle grey allotrope and a soft yellow one.

5 **B** BORON

Boron

Versatile boron is used in laundry bleaches and soaps and as a cockroach killer. Added to glass, it gives greater resistance to temperature changes. Added to steel, it gives extra hardness.

What it is	A brown powder; black crystals
Melting point	2,076°C (3,769°F)
Boiling point	3,927°C (7,101°F)

The long haul
Mule trains once hauled wagons of boron ore from US mines. This train marked the opening of a new mine in 1957.

32 **Ge** GERMANIUM

Germanium

Combined with silicon as a metal alloy, this element forms an ideal semiconductor (see opposite page) for high-speed electronic circuits. Germanium is also used to make lenses.

What it is	A brittle, silvery-white metalloid
Melting point	938.3°C (1,720.9°F)
Boiling point	2,820°C (5,108°F)

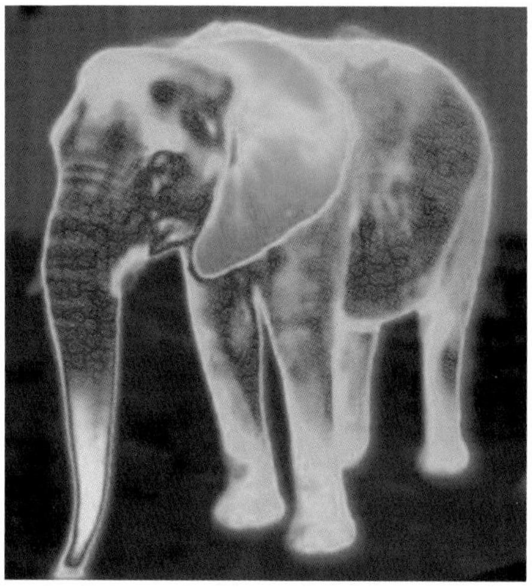

Glowing giant
Infrared cameras, which detect heat, use germanium in their lenses.

51 **Sb** ANTIMONY

Antimony

Known for thousands of years, antimony was used by the ancient Egyptians in black eye shadow and mascara. Today it is added as a hardener to metal alloys, and it is an ingredient in many flame-resistant materials.

What it is	A bright silvery metal; brittle black crystals; yellow crystals
Melting point	630.63°C (1,167.13°F)
Boiling point	1,587°C (2,889°F)

33 **As** ARSENIC

Arsenic

This element is toxic to nearly all life, apart from some tough types of bacteria. It was once a favourite poison of murderers, because its presence in a dead body was difficult to detect.

Potent poison
When taken into the body, arsenic causes organ failure.

What it is	A grey metal; a yellow non-metal; a glassy black semiconductor
Melting point	817°C (1,503°F)
Boiling point	614°C (1,137°F)

Other metalloids:

Tellurium (Te); Polonium (Po)

Drill bit
Antimony is added to metal alloys to make tough drills that can cut through rock.

Amethyst
These purple amethyst crystals are made of the compound silicon dioxide (silicon and oxygen). Tiny amounts of impurities give the crystals their colour.

14
Si
SILICON

Silicon

A major ingredient of Earth's crust, silicon is important in the manufacture of glass, ceramics, and concrete. But this metalloid is best known as a semiconductor. A semiconductor does not conduct electricity as well as a metal does, but the current it transmits can be controlled. There are tiny silicon switches in every electronic device.

What it is	A shiny grey metalloid
Melting point	1,414°C (2,577°F)
Boiling point	2,900°C (5,252°F)
Special features	Semiconductor silicon is the purest substance ever made

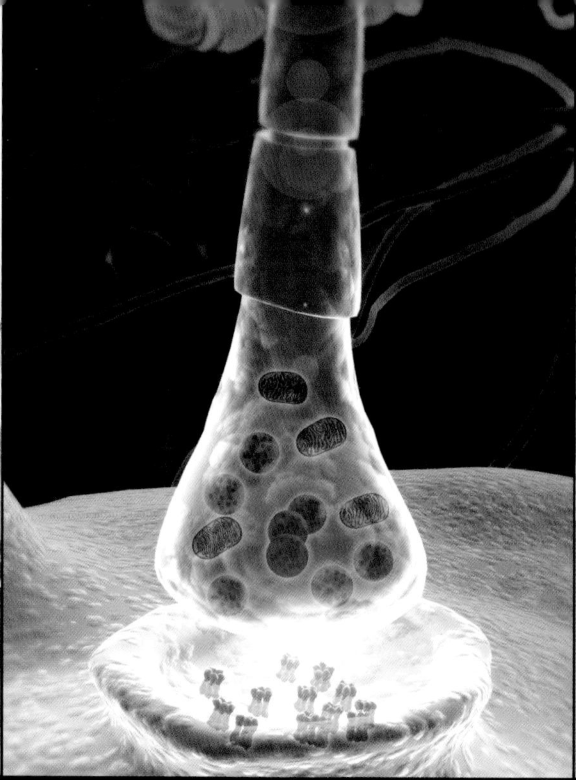

Non-m
ga

* Why do explosives go bang?
* What do elements do inside your body?
* Which element protects racing drivers from fire?

etals &

ses

Non-metals & gases

The last few groups of the periodic table are filled with non-metals, many of which are gases. Here, you will find elements essential to life – including carbon, oxygen, and nitrogen – as well as the furiously reactive halogen gases and the extremely unreactive noble gases.

Mixed bunch

The non-metals lie on the right of the periodic table. Although they are few in number, the non-metals are more varied and interesting than many metals. With significantly lower melting and boiling points than metals (excluding carbon), most of these elements are gases. They are also poor conductors of heat and electricity.

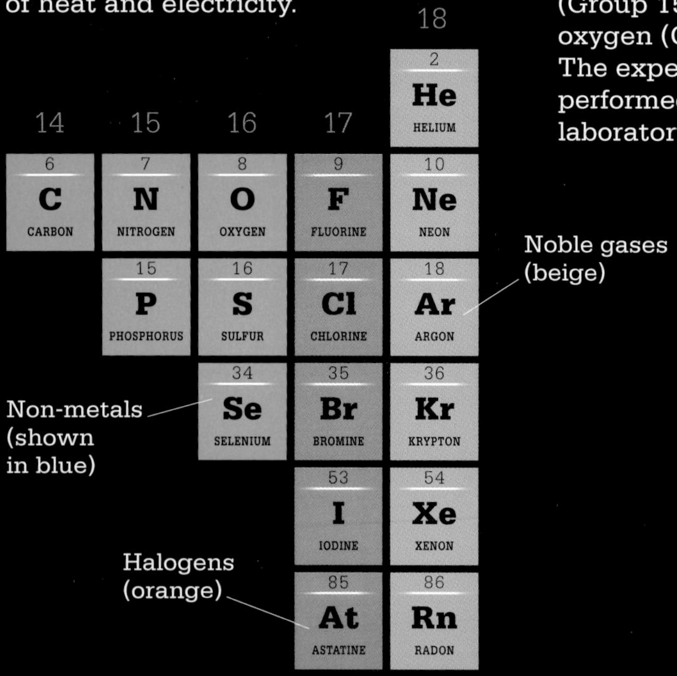

18
14
15
16
17
2 He HELIUM
6 C CARBON
7 N NITROGEN
8 O OXYGEN
9 F FLUORINE
10 Ne NEON
15 P PHOSPHORUS
16 S SULFUR
17 Cl CHLORINE
18 Ar ARGON
34 Se SELENIUM
35 Br BROMINE
36 Kr KRYPTON
53 I IODINE
54 Xe XENON
85 At ASTATINE
86 Rn RADON
Noble gases (beige)
Non-metals (shown in blue)
Halogens (orange)

WARNING! DON'T TRY THIS AT HOME

Phosphorus and oxygen

These photographs show the reaction between the non-metals phosphorus (Group 15) and oxygen (Group 16). The experiment was performed under strict laboratory conditions.

There is enough phosphorus in the human body to make 200 matches

1 A round flask is filled with pure oxygen gas. Then a small lump of the non-metal phosphorus is placed on the sand in the bottom.

2 The lump of phosphorus reacts with the oxygen in the flask. The phosphorus first begins to smoke, and soon it ignites.

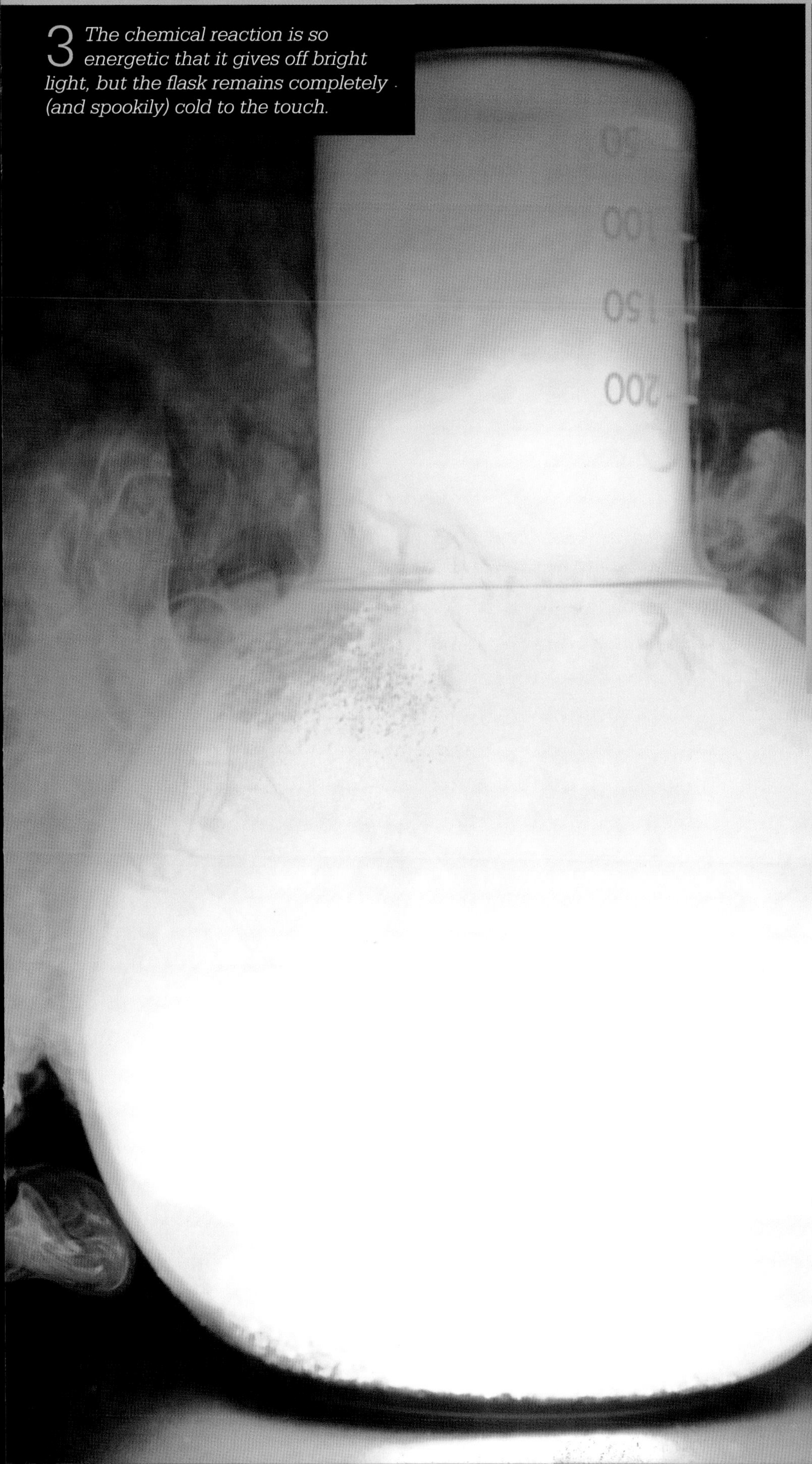

3 *The chemical reaction is so energetic that it gives off bright light, but the flask remains completely (and spookily) cold to the touch.*

4 *After the phosphorus has burned up, all that remains in the flask is smoke from the reaction. An upturned beaker keeps most of the smoke in.*

Deadly elements

Many elements are vital for life, but those that have no role in the body can be lethal once inside it. It may be a single element that wreaks havoc, or a combination of elements – such as cyanide (a substance made of carbon and nitrogen) – that does the harm.

Murder in mind

The Borgias were a ruthless family in Italy whose enemies did not last long. Lucrezia Borgia is said to have worn a hollow ring in which she kept a poison made of arsenic, phosphorus, and copper.

LUCREZIA BORGIA (1480–1519)

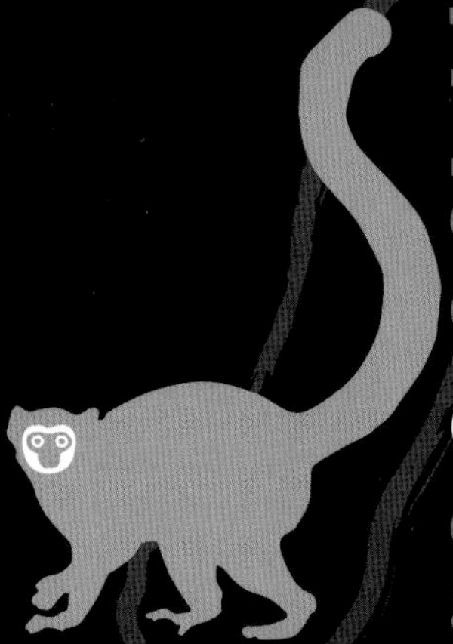

The bamboo lemur consumes enough cyanide daily to kill a human

Know your poison

When unwanted elements enter our bodies, they damage organs and change the behaviour of cells. But people did not always know about their deadly properties, and some famous folks suffered at the hands of these toxic terrors.

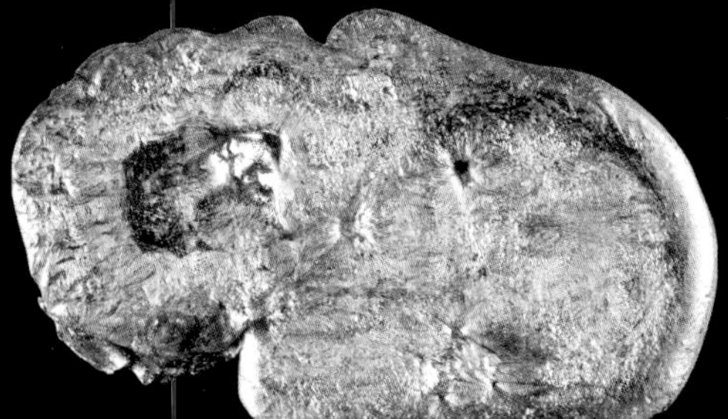

Dead from lead?

Scientists disagree about what caused the death of the composer Beethoven, but it could have been lead. He took lead-laced medicines for his ailments, and we now know that even a tiny amount of lead can damage the body.

LUDWIG VAN BEETHOVEN (1770–1827)

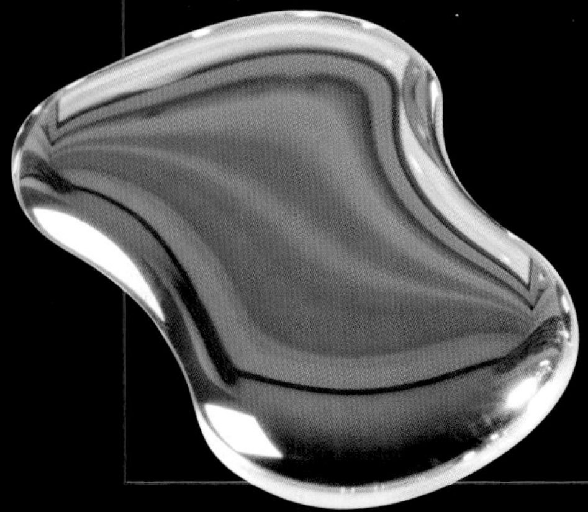

Mind-bending mercury

Abraham Lincoln, the 16th president, treated his fits of rage and depression with "little blue pills", whose main ingredient was toxic mercury. He was shot in 1865 – but if the bullet hadn't killed him, the mercury eventually would have!

ABRAHAM LINCOLN (1809–1865)

Awful arsenic

Impressionist artists of the 19th century went mad for Paris green – literally! This vivid green paint contained arsenic. Cézanne's diabetes, van Gogh's mental problems, and Monet's blindness were probably caused by this toxic paint.

CLAUDE MONET (1840–1926)

Radioactive radium

Radium kills by releasing lethal radiation into the body. Marie Curie (far right), the discoverer of radium, carried radioactive material around in her pocket, unaware of the dangers. She eventually died of radiation sickness.

MARIE CURIE (1867–1934)

Polonium peril

Not all deaths from toxic elements are accidental. The Russian ex-spy Alexander Litvinenko was murdered in London in 2006. His food was poisoned with polonium, a radioactive element, and he died three weeks later.

ALEXANDER LITVINENKO (1962–2006)

World War I military cemetery, Belgium

Chlorine was used as poison gas in World War I, carried by the wind over enemy positions. When the wind changed, it often blew the gas over the attackers instead.

91,000

soldiers died from poison gas attacks during World War I

Non-metals [Poor conductors]

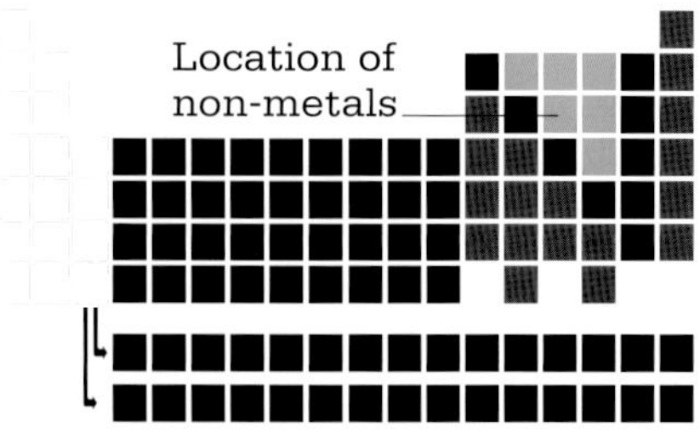
Location of non-metals
PERIODIC TABLE

There are only a few non-metals. These gases and dull, brittle materials are poor conductors of electricity and heat. But don't dismiss this bunch of elements lightly – non-metals make up most of Earth, the atmosphere, and even your body!

15
P
PHOSPHORUS

Phosphorus

There are two sides to this element. Phosphorus is used in dangerous stuff such as explosives, but it also helps build bones and form vital molecules in your body, such as the DNA in your cells.

DNA molecule
This substance contains all the instructions your body needs to grow and function.

What it is	Explosive white, red, or black non-metal
Melting point (white)	44.2°C (111.6°F)
Boiling point (white)	277°C (531°F)

Elements for growth

For healthy growth, plants need phosphorus and nitrogen, which they obtain naturally from the soil. Some farmers use fertilizers to give their crops a helping hand. The fertilizers provide extra nitrogen and phosphorus to boost plant growth.

Spreading fertilizer
Farmers sometimes use nitrogen and phosphorus in fertilizers to help their crops produce bigger harvests.

Chopped onions release sulfur compounds – they make you cry

16
S
SULFUR

Sulfur

This vile-smelling element occurs naturally near hot springs and volcanic craters. Sulfur is used to make sulfuric acid, the most important industrial chemical.

What it is	Bright yellow crystals
Melting point	115.21°C (239.38°F)
Boiling point	444.72°C (832.5°F)

Vivid and vital
Vibrant yellow sulfur is a vital element for many living organisms.

Go nuts!
A diet that includes nuts, such as Brazils, helps you maintain your selenium levels.

34
Se
SELENIUM

Selenium

Named after the Greek word for "moon", selenium is a nutrient that we need in the right amount to stay healthy. A diet low in selenium causes heart problems; too much of it can make you sick. There are semiconducting (see page 73) and non-conducting forms of selenium.

What it is	Purplish-grey semi-metal; also glassy black and crystalline red
Melting point	221°C (430°F)
Boiling point	685°C (1,265°F)

Other non-metals:

Carbon (C); Oxygen (O)

7
N
NITROGEN

Nitrogen

When nitrogen atoms link up with those of other elements, they sometimes form explosive compounds – the "N" in TNT stands for "nitro". Fortunately, the nitrogen gas in the air is unreactive. This is because it is in the form of molecular nitrogen – pairs of nitrogen atoms held tightly together by chemical bonds.

What it is	Colourless, inert gas
Melting point	–210.1°C (–346.18°F)
Boiling point	–195.79°C (–320.42°F)
Special features	Colourless, odourless, and tasteless

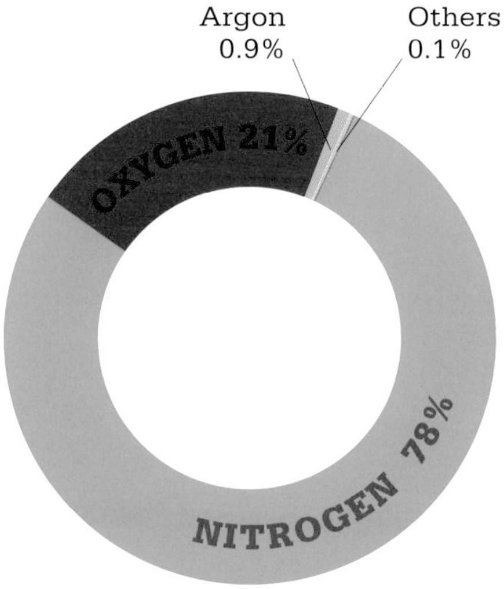
Argon 0.9%
Others 0.1%
OXYGEN 21%
NITROGEN 78%

Composition of air
Nearly 80 per cent of the air is nitrogen gas, giving Earth a stable, unreactive atmosphere that allows life to flourish.

The atmosphere of Titan, Saturn's largest moon, is 98% nitrogen

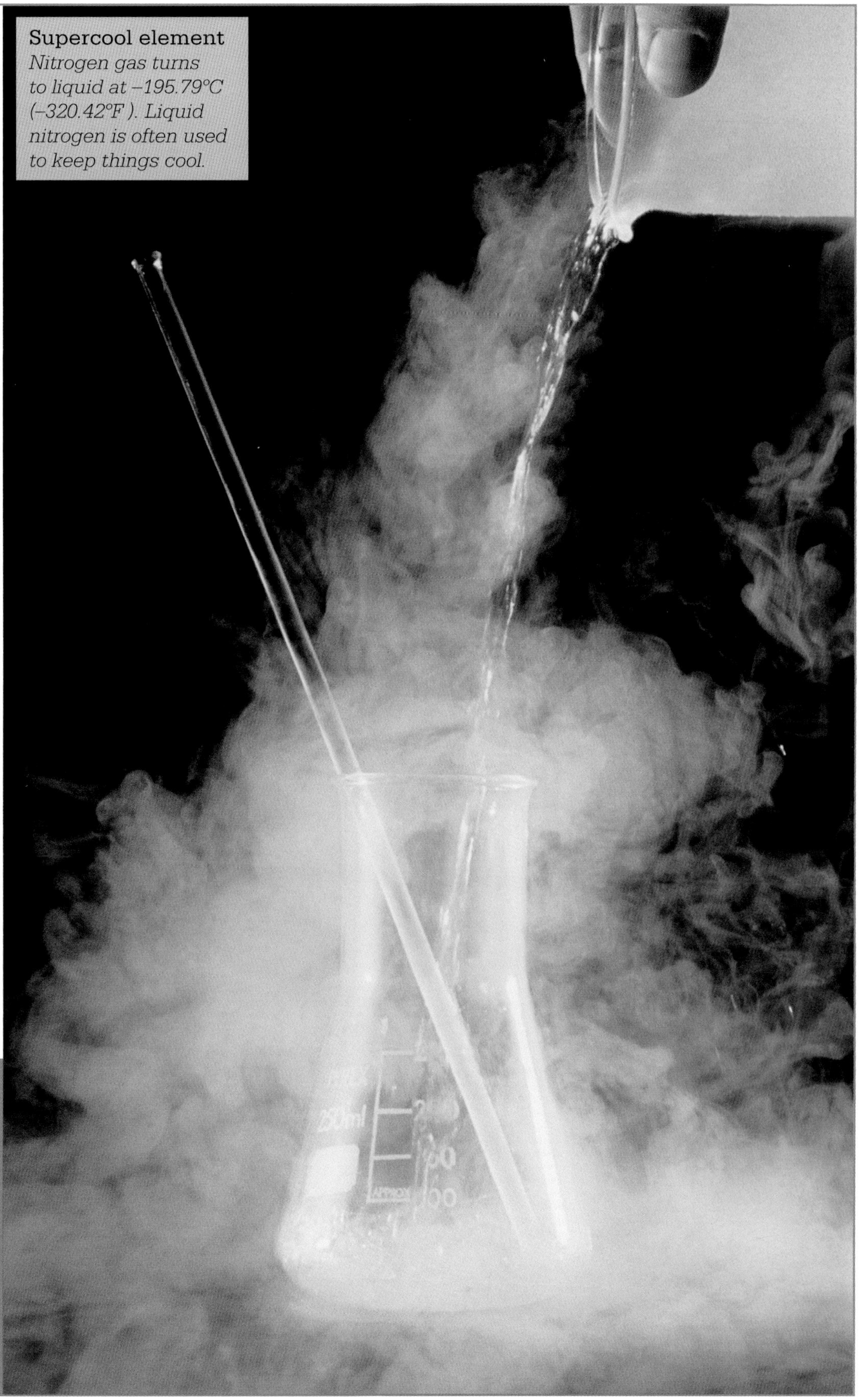

Supercool element
Nitrogen gas turns to liquid at –195.79°C (–320.42°F). Liquid nitrogen is often used to keep things cool.

Oxygen [The spark of life]

8
O
OXYGEN

As a component of water, oxygen covers most of the planet's surface and is vital for life. And as a gas that makes up 21 per cent of the air that you breathe, oxygen drives chemical processes in your body. This reactive element is also at the heart of every fire that burns.

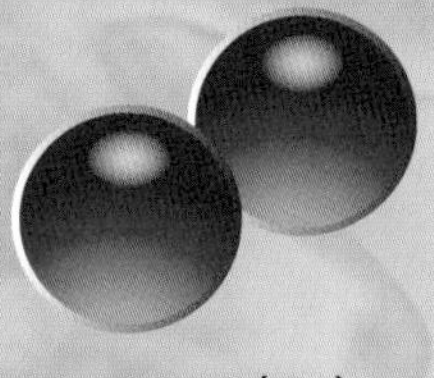

Oxygen (O_2)
An oxygen gas molecule is made up of two linked oxygen atoms.

Element profile

Name	Oxygen
Symbol	O
Atomic number	8
What it is	A colourless, odourless gas
Melting point	–218.3°C (–360.9°F)
Boiling point	–182.9°C (–297.2°F)
Special features	Most common element in Earth's crust; essential for life; light blue as a liquid

Giant dragonfly fossil
Around 300 million years ago, atmospheric oxygen reached a peak of 35 per cent, allowing insects, such as Meganeura, *to grow to giant sizes.*

Meganeura*'s wingspan was over 75 cm (2.5 ft).*

Ancient air

The atmosphere of the young Earth would have been deadly to us, since it contained no oxygen. Gradually, oxygen began to build up in the air as it was released by ocean life-forms called blue-green algae.

Oxygen in the atmosphere began building up 2.5 billion years ago

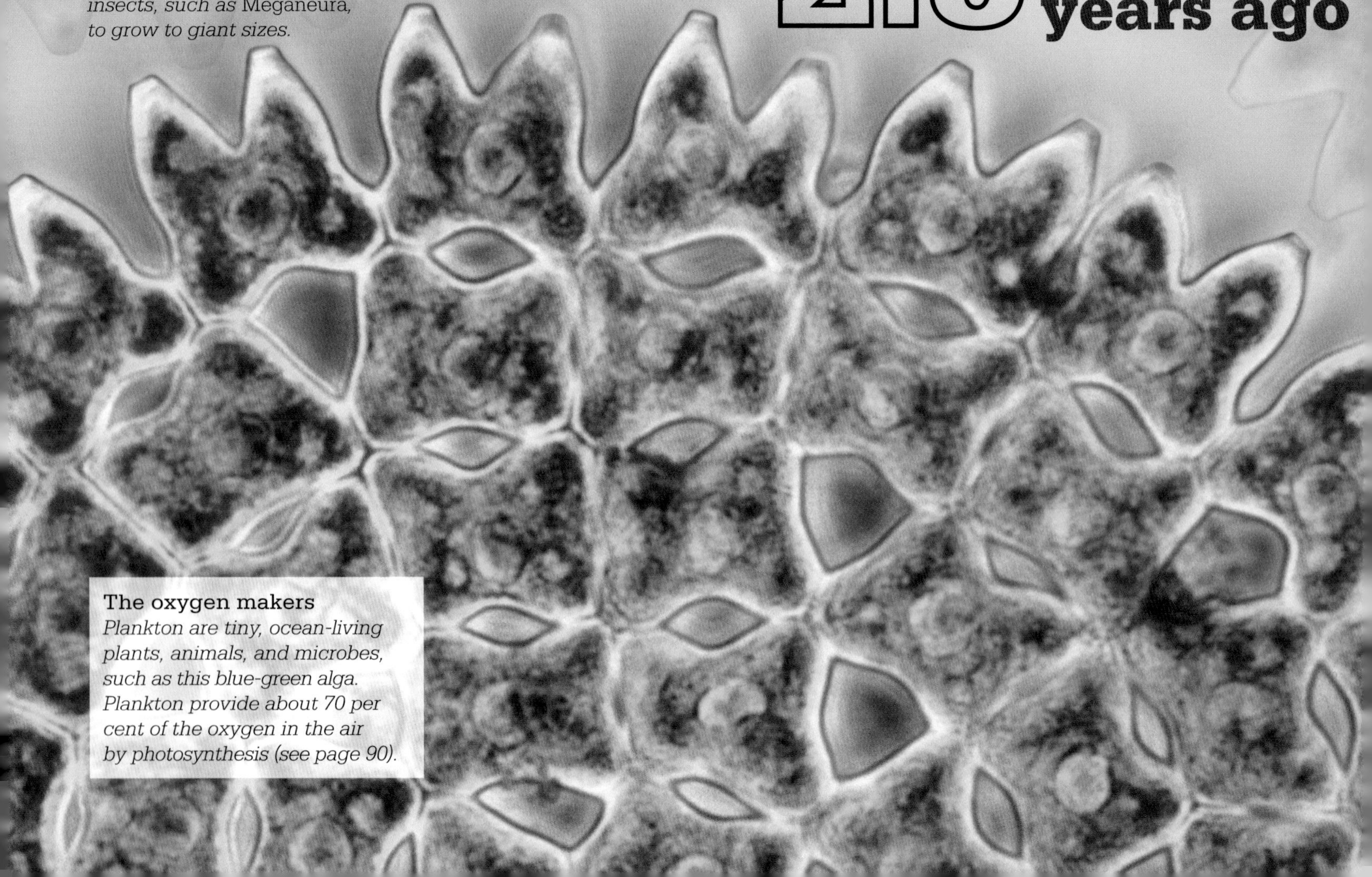

The oxygen makers
Plankton are tiny, ocean-living plants, animals, and microbes, such as this blue-green alga. Plankton provide about 70 per cent of the oxygen in the air by photosynthesis (see page 90).

The great reactor

Oxygen is very reactive. Burning, for example, is a reaction between a substance, such as wood, and oxygen in the air. Because of oxygen's reactivity, most of Earth's oxygen is locked up in the crust, bound to other elements as oxide compounds.

Wildfire
When there is an abundant supply of oxygen and plenty of material to burn, it's difficult to stop a fire.

Making oxygen

The oxygen needed for industrial processes such as steelmaking (see page 58) is obtained from air by a process known as distillation. This "manufactured" oxygen is also used in hospitals and aircraft.

Life-saving gas
Manufactured oxygen allows astronauts, mountain climbers, and divers to breathe in extreme and dangerous environments.

Wrapped in gas

Earth's atmosphere is mostly oxygen and nitrogen, with small amounts of other gases. There are layers within the atmosphere, each with a different temperature and a slightly different mix of gases. The ozone layer is rich in a form of oxygen called ozone.

OZONE MOLECULE

Ozone (O_3)
An ozone molecule consists of three oxygen atoms. The ozone layer protects living things from the Sun's harmful ultraviolet (UV) rays.

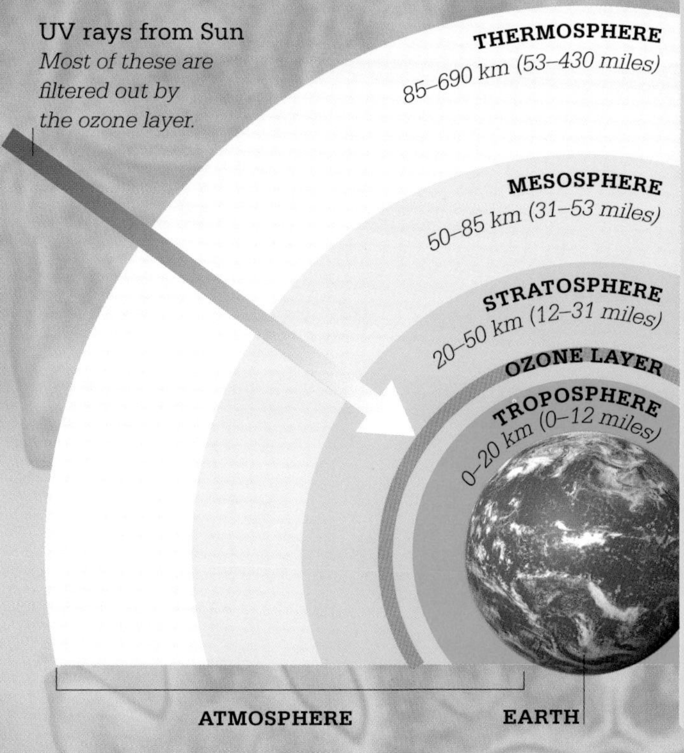
THERMOSPHERE
85–690 km (53–430 miles)
MESOSPHERE
50–85 km (31–53 miles)
STRATOSPHERE
20–50 km (12–31 miles)
OZONE LAYER
TROPOSPHERE
0–20 km (0–12 miles)
ATMOSPHERE
EARTH

UV rays from Sun
Most of these are filtered out by the ozone layer.

More here

ozone layer forest fire cyanobacteria **plankton** **stromatolite** respiration combustion **death zone** **water** liquid oxygen atmosphere **ultraviolet** **distillation** *Meganeura*

Get experimenting!
To see how burning relies on oxygen, ask an adult to place an upturned glass jar over a lighted candle. The flame will go out, but only after it has used up all the oxygen in the jar.

burning: a chemical reaction in which a substance combines with oxygen, releasing heat.

distillation: the process of heating a liquid mixture to separate out its components. To distil air, the air has to first be cooled so that it turns into a liquid.

photosynthesis: the process by which plants use the energy in sunlight to make food from carbon dioxide and water. Oxygen is released as a waste product (see pages 90–91).

Human body [What makes

Your body is a complex blend of many compounds of the elements, which work together to keep you healthy and safe from harm. For trouble-free operation, your body needs about 33 elements, but many of them only in minuscule quantities.

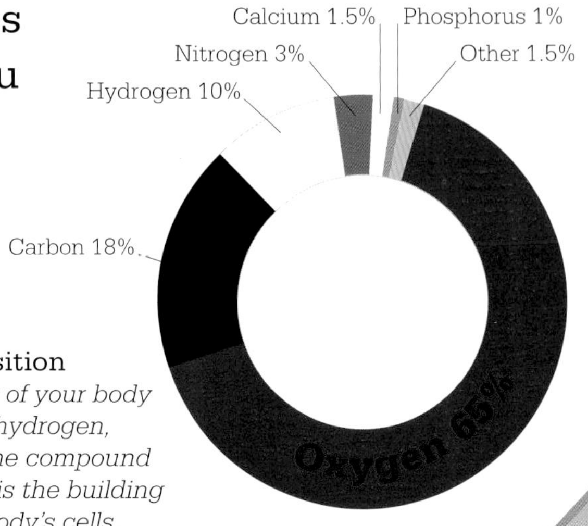

Calcium 1.5%
Phosphorus 1%
Nitrogen 3%
Other 1.5%
Hydrogen 10%
Carbon 18%
Oxygen 65%

Body composition
Three-quarters of your body is oxygen and hydrogen, combined as the compound water. Carbon is the building block of your body's cells.

The elements inside

In an average adult, there are about 50 kilograms (110 pounds) of water (oxygen and hydrogen), 18 kilograms (40 pounds) of carbon (see page 88), several kilograms of calcium, a little nitrogen and phosphorus, and some iron. In addition to these major elements, there are also "micronutrients" – tiny amounts of elements such as zinc, iodine, manganese, and selenium.

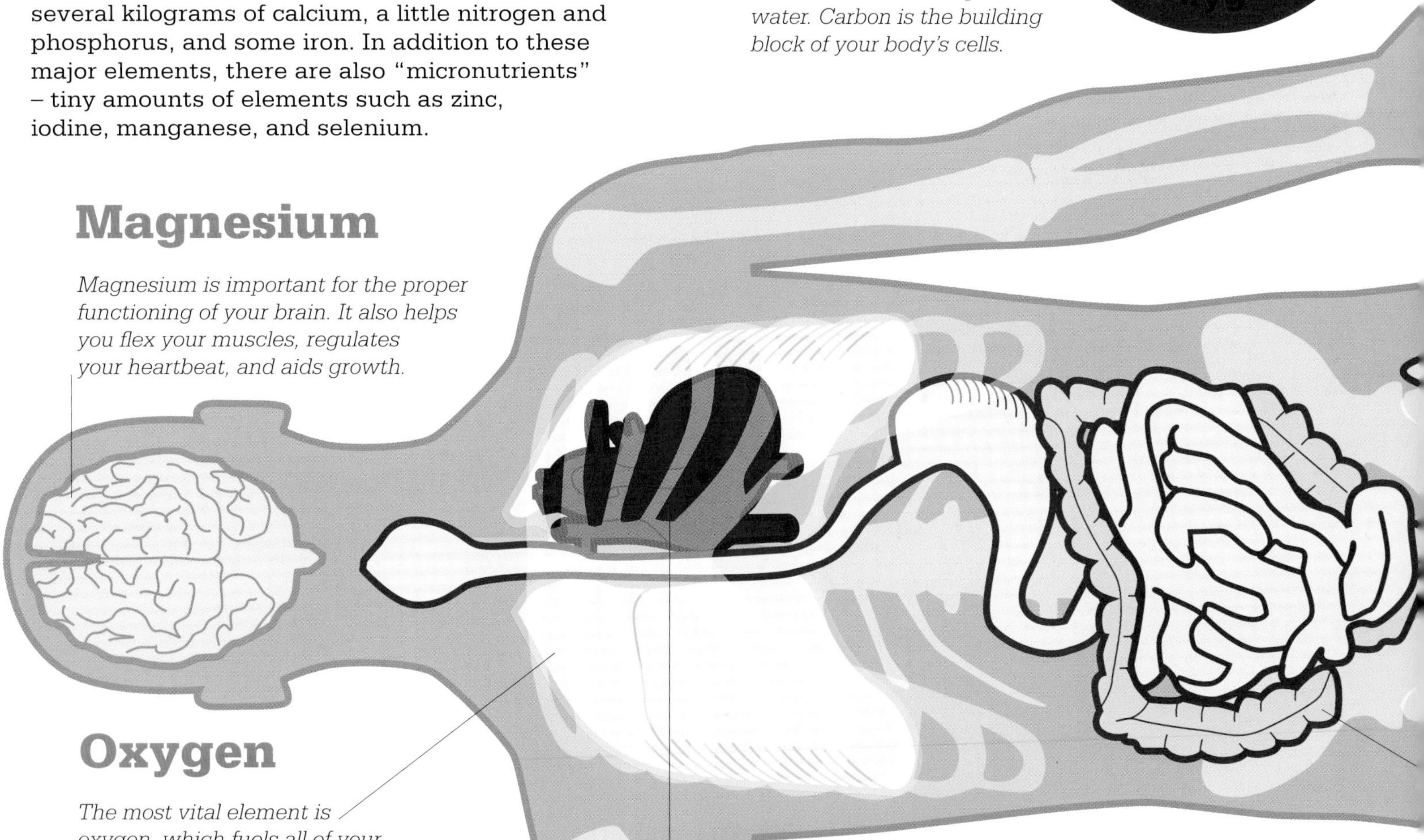

Magnesium

Magnesium is important for the proper functioning of your brain. It also helps you flex your muscles, regulates your heartbeat, and aids growth.

Oxygen

The most vital element is oxygen, which fuels all of your body's chemical reactions. You draw it into your lungs as you take in each breath of air.

Iron

Iron is part of the haemoglobin molecules in red blood cells. Oxygen taken in by the lungs is delivered by these molecules to every cell of your body.

Red blood cells
Your body needs two-millionths of a gram of iron every day to make new red blood cells.

Your body contains enough iron to make a 7.5-cm (3-in) nail

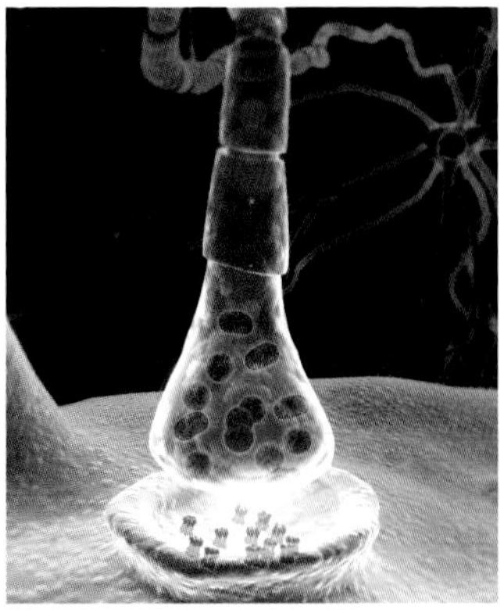

NERVE CELLS SIGNALLING, AIDED BY POTASSIUM

Phosphorus

This element is a key ingredient of bones and the DNA molecules found in your cells (see page 80). It is also part of the substance ATP, which drives your muscles.

Calcium

Your bones and teeth are made of calcium phosphate (see page 38). Calcium helps muscles to grow and blood to clot, and regulates blood pressure.

Potassium

Potassium helps keep your body chemistry in balance. It also plays a leading role in sending signals between nerve cells throughout your body.

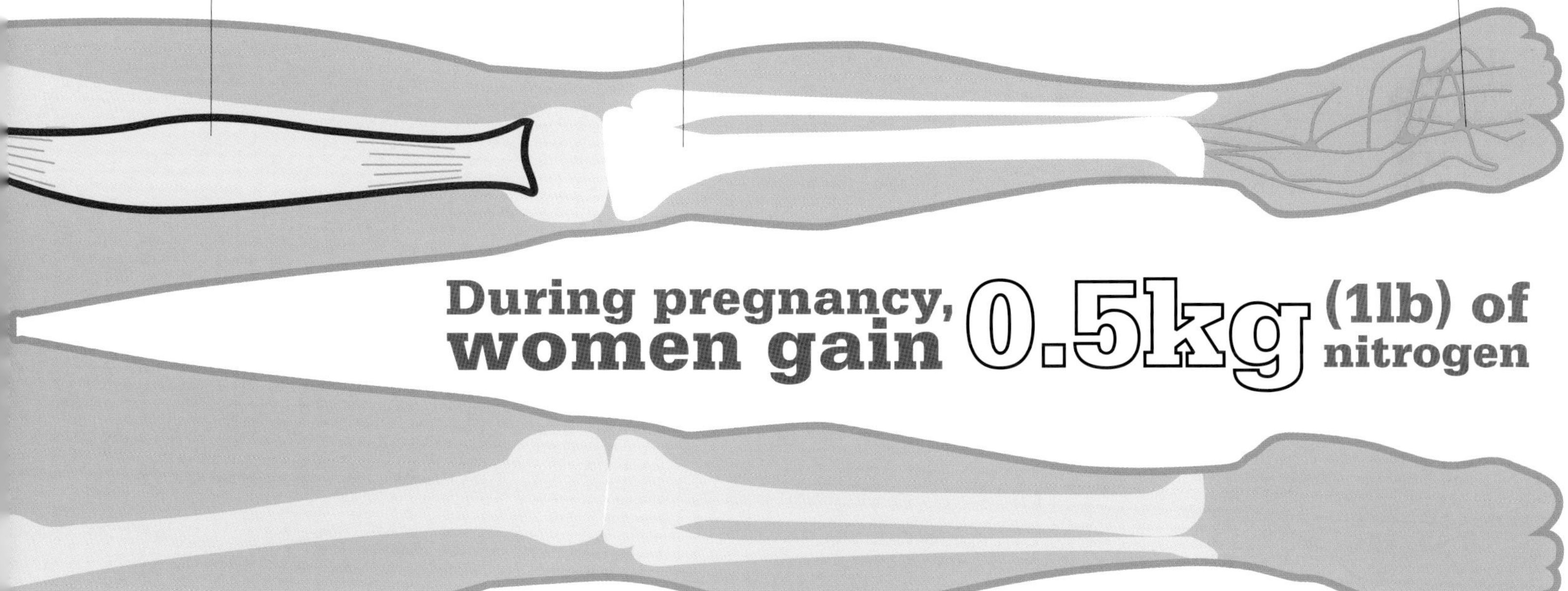

During pregnancy, women gain 0.5kg (1lb) of nitrogen

Nitrogen

Nitrogen is found in many essential body chemicals, such as proteins and amino acids. Enzymes made from nitrogen-containing amino acids help you digest food.

Digestion

Enzymes break down large food molecules into smaller molecules that are easier for your body to absorb and use. Carbohydrase is an enzyme that splits starch into simple sugars.

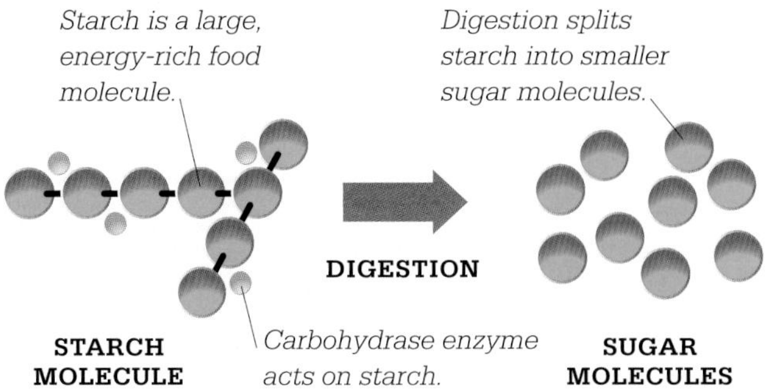
Starch is a large, energy-rich food molecule.
Digestion splits starch into smaller sugar molecules.
DIGESTION
STARCH MOLECULE
Carbohydrase enzyme acts on starch.
SUGAR MOLECULES

Elements in sports

In track cycling, good equipment is crucial – anything that shaves a second off your time can make you a winner! Bikes have lightweight carbon-fibre frames moulded into streamlined shapes. Strong aluminium alloy is used for the wheels. The hard carbon-fibre shell of the padded helmet gives vital protection when you're pedalling at 85 kilometres per hour (53 miles per hour) with no brakes, and another cyclist is just centimetres behind you!

Carbon [It's got the power!]

6
C
CARBON

The vast majority of known compounds contain carbon. This element is so good at forming compounds because each carbon atom can link with up to four other atoms. Carbon compounds are the basis of life, and they provide us with fuels and other useful materials.

Element profile

Name	Carbon
Symbol	C
Atomic number	6
What it is	A black or clear non-metal solid
Melting point	3,500°C (6,400°F)
Boiling point	4,027°C (7,281°F)
Special features	Forms big molecules that are essential to living things

Natural carbon

Carbon can occur naturally in different forms, known as allotropes (see page 72). Sparkling diamond, which is the hardest of all natural substances, is pure carbon. So, too, is the soft graphite used for pencil "lead".

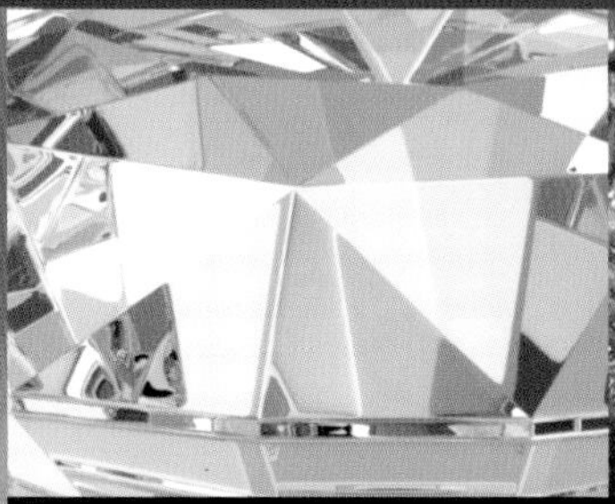

DIAMOND

GRAPHITE

The energizers

Carbohydrates, such as sugars and starches, are compounds of carbon, hydrogen, and oxygen. Carbohydrates supply animals and plants with energy to fuel their body processes.

Carbon-based life

Most of your body tissues are made up of carbon-containing proteins, carbohydrates, and fats. Carbon also forms the backbone of the DNA molecule (see page 80) found in all your cells.

Living carbon
Almost every part of your body contains the element carbon.

Carbohydrates in food
Starchy foods, such as cereals, bread, potatoes, rice, beans, and pasta, are packed with energy-giving carbohydrates.

Fossil fuels

Coal, crude oil, and natural gas are called fossil fuels. This is because they are formed from the fossilized, carbon-rich remains of long-dead plants and animals. When we burn these fuels, they release lots of energy, which we can use to generate electricity, power industry, and fuel our cars.

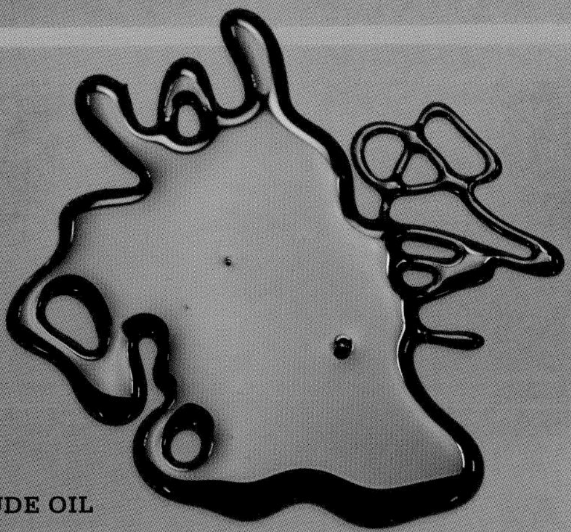

CRUDE OIL

80% of the energy we use comes from burning fossil fuels

Environmental impact

Burning fossil fuels produces polluting gases that are dangerous to our health and to the environment. They also absorb heat and warm the planet. This "global warming" is threatening to upset the balance of life on Earth (see page 91).

Oil refinery
Working around the clock, oil refineries produce fuels and chemicals essential for industry.

Products from oil

Crude oil is a liquid mix of hydrocarbons (hydrogen-carbon compounds). Refineries heat oil until it turns to gas. As the gas cools, the different hydrocarbons in the mixture condense back to liquids at different temperatures.

COOL | SUBSTANCE

Liquid petroleum gas, below 20°C (70°F)
Used for cooking and for making plastics.

Oil, 20°C–70°C (70°F–160°F)
An explosive fuel used in car engines.

Naphtha, 70°C–160°C (160°F–320°F)
A yellow liquid used for making chemicals.

Kerosene, 160°C–250°C (320°F–480°F)
A light, oily liquid used for jet fuel.

Diesel, 250°C–350°C (480°F–660°F)
Liquid fuel used in some engines.

Fuel oil, 350°C–380°C (660°F–715°F)
Heavy fuel for ships and power stations.

Lubricating oil and bitumen, over 380°C (715°F)
Grease, lubricants, and tar for road-building and roofing.

HOT

Carbon for life [The key cycle]

Combined with oxygen as the gas carbon dioxide (CO_2), carbon is present in Earth's atmosphere. Plants need this CO_2 to make their food. All animals eat either plants or other plant-eating animals. So without CO_2, there would be no life on Earth.

Sucking up carbon

Plants get the carbon they need to build their "bodies" directly from the air. Using energy from the Sun, they turn CO_2 and water into glucose (a simple sugar molecule) by a process called photosynthesis.

WATER FROM ROOTS

Leafy business
Photosynthesis takes place inside the leaves of plants. It uses water taken up by the roots and CO_2 absorbed from the air.

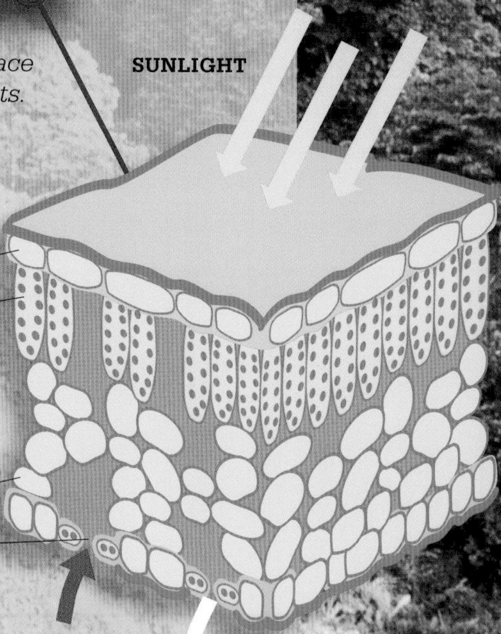

SUNLIGHT
Surface cells
Chloroplasts
Sugar-making cells
Leaf pores
CARBON DIOXIDE IN
OXYGEN OUT

Chloroplasts
The Sun's energy is captured by tiny structures in the plant cell called chloroplasts.

Leaf pores
Holes on the underside allow CO_2 to enter the leaf and oxygen (a waste product of photosynthesis) to escape.

Building with sugar
The glucose sugar made in the leaves provides food for the plant. It is also converted into a substance called cellulose, which is used to build plant cells.

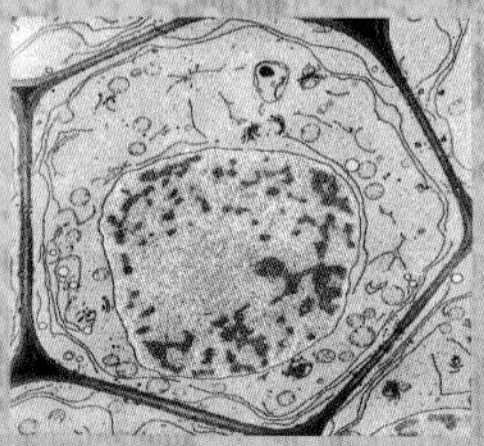
PLANT CELL

Greenhouse effect

Carbon dioxide and other gases in the atmosphere warm Earth by trapping the Sun's heat, just like a greenhouse does. Without these gases, Earth would be a freezing −18°C (−0.4°F) and too cold for life.

EARTH FROM SPACE

The carbon cycle

Carbon, in the form of CO_2, circulates naturally between the atmosphere, living things, and the land and oceans.

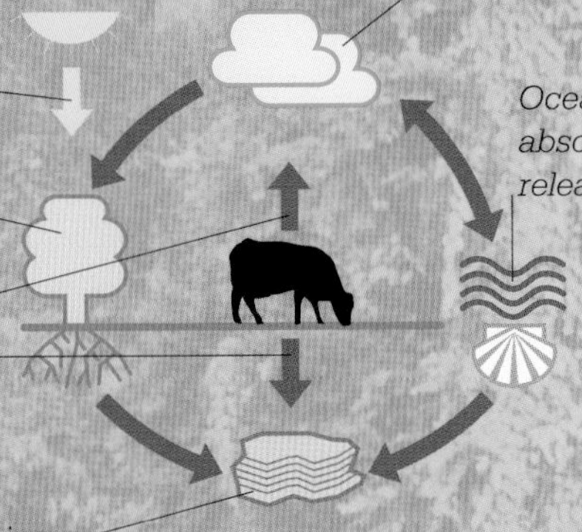
CO_2 in the atmosphere
Photosynthesis
Green plants absorb CO_2.
Animals eat plants and breathe out CO_2.
Plants and animals die and their remains are incorporated into the ground.
Plant and animal remains form fossil fuels.
Oceans absorb and release CO_2.

Too much CO2

When a fossil fuel (see page 89) burns, carbon locked up in the fuel combines with oxygen to form CO_2, which escapes into the air. We are adding so much extra CO_2 into the atmosphere that Earth is overheating.

6 C CARBON + 8 O OXYGEN 8 O OXYGEN = CO_2

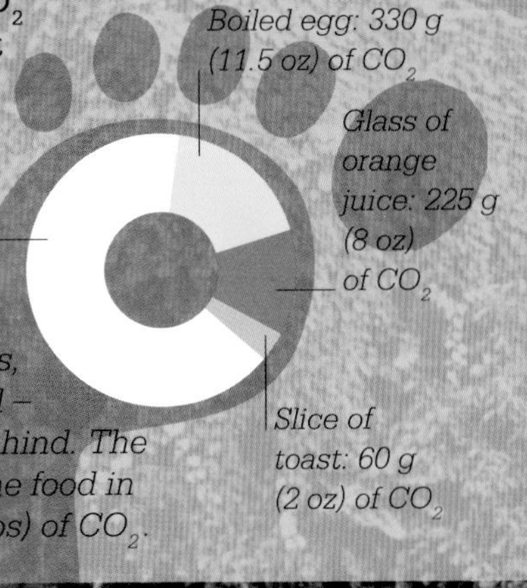
Boiled egg: 330 g (11.5 oz) of CO_2
Glass of orange juice: 225 g (8 oz) of CO_2
Cereal and milk: 1.2 kg (2.6 lbs) of CO_2
Slice of toast: 60 g (2 oz) of CO_2

Carbon footprint

Every time we use fossil fuels, an amount of CO_2 is released – a "carbon footprint" is left behind. The footprint left by producing the food in this breakfast is 1.8 kg (3.9 lbs) of CO_2.

Capturing carbon

Rainforests, such as this one in Borneo, collect huge amounts of carbon as they absorb CO_2. They also release a lot of oxygen gas into the atmosphere.

Halogens [Caution required!]

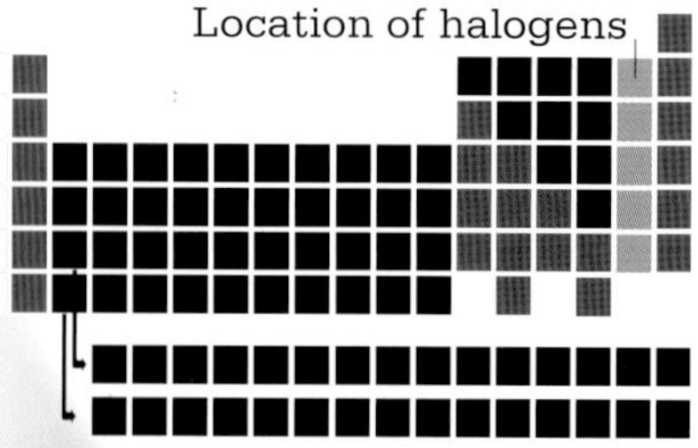

PERIODIC TABLE

Everything about the halogens is intense. This is a group of colourful, feisty, non-metallic elements on the right of the periodic table. The halogens react violently with most things, and it takes a lot of energy to break up the compounds that they form.

Evaporating iodine
When heated, iodine quickly evaporates to form a beautiful purple gas.

Iodine

53 **I** IODINE

Make sure you eat your greens – they contain lots of iodine, which helps your body to develop healthily. Iodine is also a great antiseptic, used to keep wounds free from infection.

What it is	A purplish-black solid
Melting point	113.7°C (236.66°F)
Boiling point	184.3°C (363.7°F)

Chlorine

17 **Cl** CHLORINE

Chlorine can be lethal to living things. But tiny amounts of chlorine are added to drinking water to kill germs. It has saved millions of people from dying of waterborne diseases such as cholera and typhoid.

What it is	A pale green gas
Melting point	–101.5°C (–150.7°F)
Boiling point	–34.04°C (–29.27°F)

Swimming smell
Chlorine kills germs in pools, but its smell lingers in the water.

Bromine

35 **Br** BROMINE

Brown bromine stinks – its name comes from the Greek for "stench of goats"! Known since ancient times, it was an ingredient of the purple colour worn by the rulers of Rome. Bromine occurs in large quantities in the Dead Sea.

RACING-CAR DRIVER IN FIREPROOF SUIT

Liquid brown
Although liquid at room temperature, bromine is always on the point of turning into a foul-smelling gas.

Flame fighter
Bromine compounds are great at resisting flames, so they are used in fireproof materials.

What it is	A smoking, red-brown liquid
Melting point	–7.3°C (19°F)
Boiling point	59°C (138°F)

The colour thief
In the presence of water, chlorine makes short work of bright colours.

1 *A wet, bright red flower is placed into a jar of chlorine gas. There is a rapid reaction.*

2 *The chlorine bleaches the colour from the flower, turning it almost white.*

30 g (1 oz) of astatine exists in the crust of Earth

Astatine

85 **At** ASTATINE

One of the world's rarest elements, astatine only forms from the radioactive decay (see pages 64–65) of other elements. Astatine quickly decays after it forms – then it's gone again! It was first made artificially in 1947.

What it is	A radioactive black solid
Melting point	302°C (576°F)
Boiling point	337°C (639°F)

Fluorite crystals
Halogens react violently with metals to form stable compounds called salts. These crystals of fluorite are an example of a salt formed by fluorine with calcium.

9
F
FLUORINE

Fluorine

Fluorine gas readily bursts into flame, and it attacks any vessel it is kept in. Because of this, it can form stable (unreactive) compounds. Fluorine compounds are put in toothpaste to protect teeth. They also form non-stick coatings for skis and cooking pans.

What it is	A yellow-green gas
Melting point	–219.62°C (–363.32°F)
Boiling point	–188.12°C (–306.62°F)
Special features	The most reactive element in the Universe

Noble gases [Lighting up

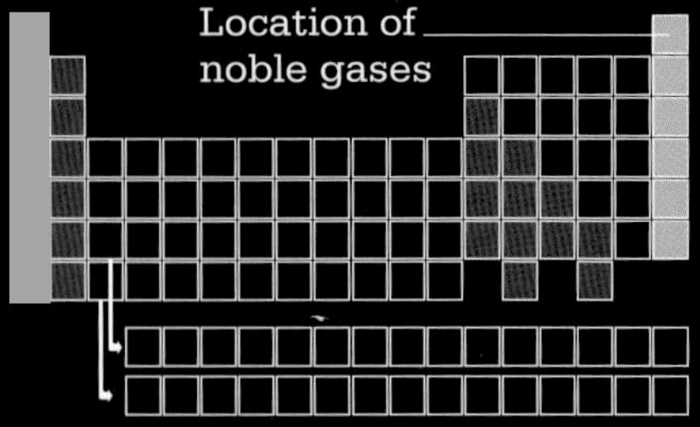
Location of noble gases

PERIODIC TABLE

These "shy" gases, which make up about one per cent of Earth's atmosphere, rarely combine with other elements. They are all colourless and odourless, but when given a chance to shine they can be dazzling!

Neon

10
Ne
NEON

Like all noble gases, neon glows when electricity passes through it. Neon lights blaze bright red-orange, bringing glamour and glitz to city nightlife.

What it is	Colourless, unreactive gas
Melting point	–248.59°C (–415.46°F)
Boiling point	–246.08°C (–410.94°F)

City lights
The first neon lights were made in the 1900s. They changed the look of cities forever.

Radon

86
Rn
RADON

This noble gas is radioactive. Radon gas is produced by the radioactive decay (see pages 64–65) of uranium in Earth's crust, and it seeps naturally out of the ground.

What it is	A radioactive gas
Melting point	–71°C (–96°F)
Boiling point	–61.7°C (–79.1°F)

HeNeArKrXe

HELIUM GAS GLOWING · NEON GAS GLOWING · ARGON GAS GLOWING · KRYPTON GAS GLOWING · XENON GAS GLOWING

Argon

18
Ar
ARGON

Unreactive argon is used in traditional light bulbs, which heat a filament – a coil of tungsten wire – until it glows. The argon stops the filament from burning out.

What it is	Unreactive gas
Melting point	–189.3°C (–308.7°F)
Boiling point	–185.8°C (–302.4°F)

Welding metals together
Argon is so unreactive that it is used to prevent explosions from taking place during dangerous work, such as welding.

Xenon

54
Xe
XENON

This gas glows pale violet under electric current. Xenon is used in the super-bright, high-temperature headlamps of many expensive cars.

Dazzle danger
Headlamps that use xenon give excellent night visibility, but they can dazzle other road users.

What it is	Unreactive, heavy gas
Melting point	–111.7°C (–169.1°F)
Boiling point	–108°C (–162°F)

Krypton

36
Kr
KRYPTON

Under electric current, krypton glows a whitish-mauve colour. Krypton is the main gas used in low-energy fluorescent lights.

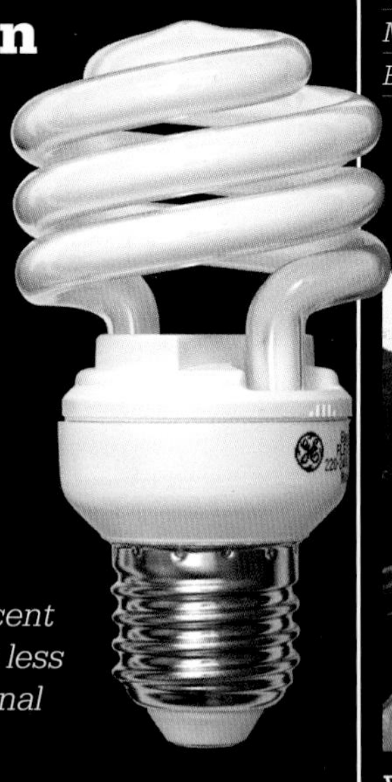

Energy saver
Low-energy fluorescent lights use five times less energy than traditional filament lightbulbs.

What it is	An unreactive, heavier-than-air gas
Melting point	–157.36°C (–251.25°F)
Boiling point	–153.22°C (–243.8°F)

24% of the mass of elements in our galaxy is helium

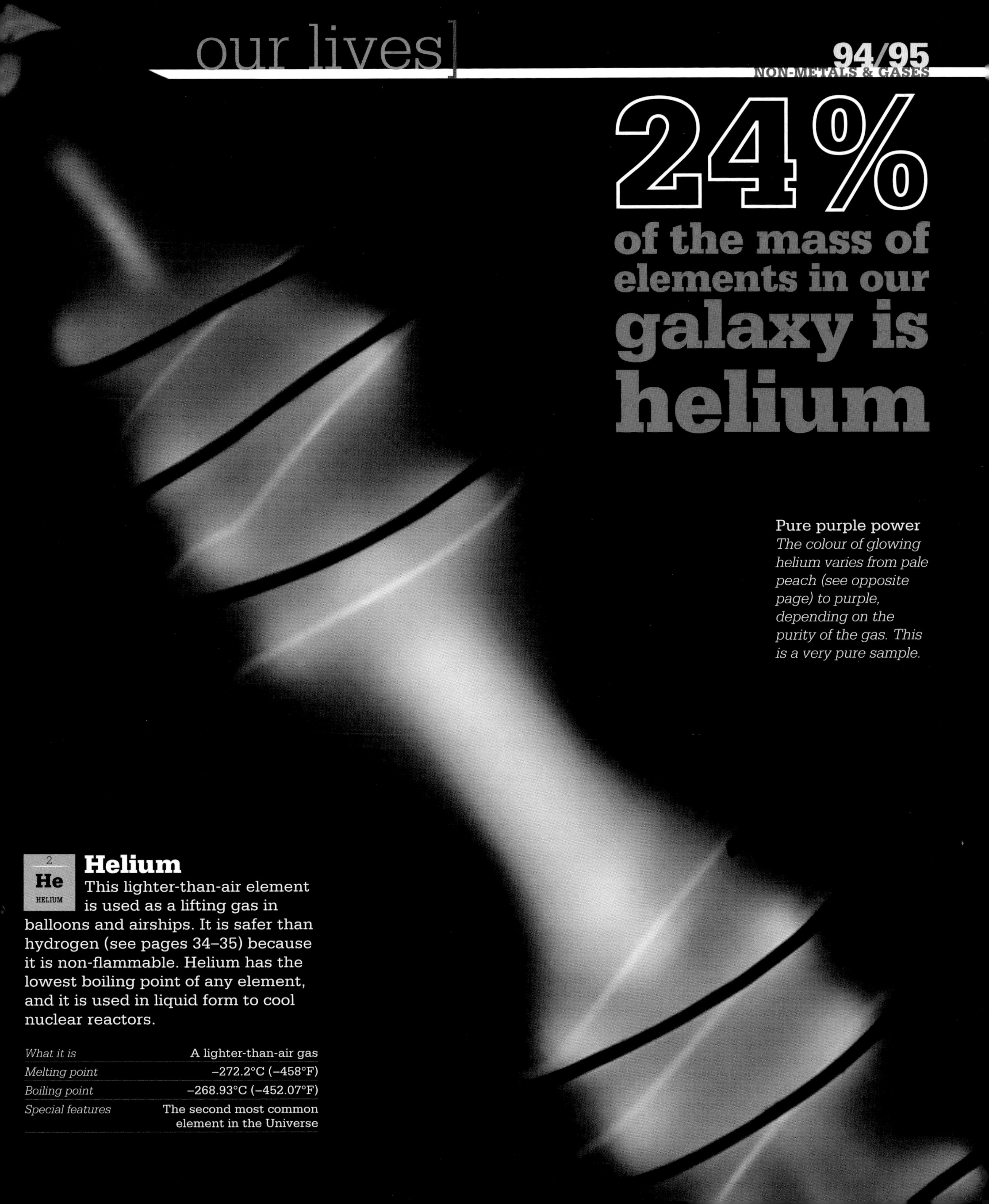

Pure purple power
The colour of glowing helium varies from pale peach (see opposite page) to purple, depending on the purity of the gas. This is a very pure sample.

Helium

2
He
HELIUM

This lighter-than-air element is used as a lifting gas in balloons and airships. It is safer than hydrogen (see pages 34–35) because it is non-flammable. Helium has the lowest boiling point of any element, and it is used in liquid form to cool nuclear reactors.

What it is	A lighter-than-air gas
Melting point	–272.2°C (–458°F)
Boiling point	–268.93°C (–452.07°F)
Special features	The second most common element in the Universe

Recycling elements

Earth has a limited supply of elements, and most are locked up inside minerals in its rocky crust. Extracting elements from their minerals requires energy, so it makes sense to recycle them rather than produce fresh material. For example, recycling just one aluminium can save enough energy to run a TV for three hours.

Many elements can be recovered from old electronics. The tracks of circuit boards are copper, while gold and silver are often used for circuit connectors. Computer screens contain silicon and lead, and silicon is also in microchips. Laptop batteries contain lithium, or nickel and cadmium, plus mercury. Tin, lead, iron, aluminium, and titanium are also in electronic devices.

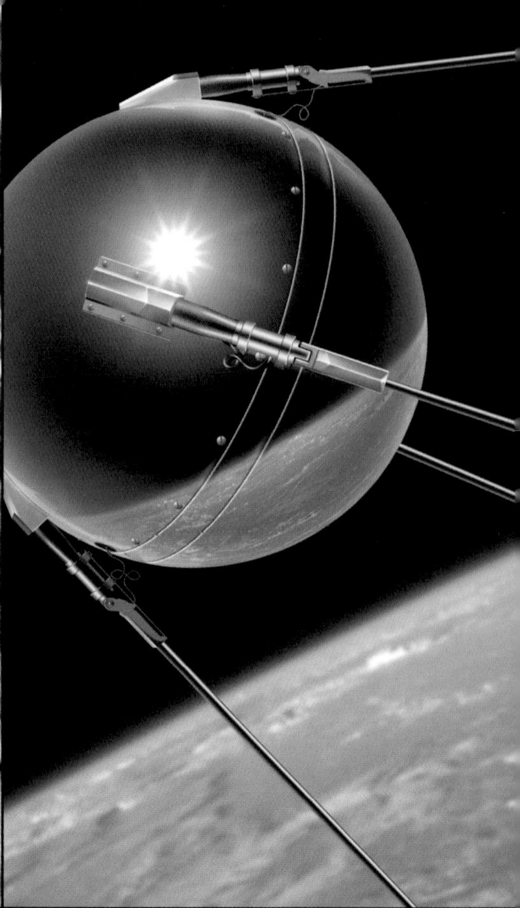

Histo
disco

* Who first described elements?
* Where was the largest gold nugget found?
* Which early space vehicle was made with titanium?

ry of
very

Element quest [Getting to

From the earliest civilizations right up until the present time, the world's greatest minds have struggled with two basic questions: What are the simplest and purest parts of matter? And how many of them are there?

Fire
Hot and dry element
Air
Hot and wet element
Earth
Cold and dry element
Water
Cold and wet element

28,000–22,000 BCE

Cave painting

During the Stone Age, colourful manganese compounds are used to make cave paintings.

3300 BCE

The Bronze Age begins when copper extracted from rocks is mixed with tin.

1300 BCE

The Iron Age starts as people learn how to extract iron from its rocky ore.

• 1000 BCE

900–350 BCE

Manganese in the iron ore used by the Spartans makes their weapons superior.

450 BCE

Greek elements

Philosophers in ancient Greece believe that just four simple substances combine to make everything: earth, fire, air, and water.

360 BCE

The word element *is used for the first time by Plato, the Greek philosopher.*

1–300 CE

Lead pipes bring water to Roman towns. The Romans do not realize that lead is toxic.

c.721–c.815 CE

Jãbir ibn Hayyãn

The Arabian alchemist (early chemist) Jãbir ibn Hayyãn finds that some substances can be broken down into simpler components, but others, such as gold and silver, always stay the same.

JÃBIR IBN HAYYÃN WITH HIS ALCHEMY EQUIPMENT

900 CE •

904 CE

Armies in China use gunpowder made of potassium nitrate and sulfur in their "flying fire" arrows.

• 1200 CE

1280

Philosopher's stone

Albertus Magnus, a friar, is rumoured to have discovered a substance that can change ordinary metals into gold.

GOLD NUGGET

• 1300

14th century

Glassworks

The glassmakers of Venice begin to use compounds of copper, cobalt, and manganese to add colours to their beautiful glass.

VENETIAN GLASS

JOSEPH PRIESTLEY
English champion
Invented: soda water
Discovered: 6 gases; 1 element

1774
Priestley vs. Lavoisier

Scientific showdown! French chemist Antoine Lavoisier uses English scientist Joseph Priestley's methods and claims to have found a new element. Priestley gets the credit, but Lavoisier gets to name the element oxygen.

ANTOINE LAVOISIER
French champion
Invented: a new scientific basis for chemistry

1783
First flight

In France, the first piloted flight of a hydrogen-filled balloon takes place.

1425
Barsbay, the Mamluk sultan of Egypt, brings in a pure gold coin known as an ashrafi.

1714
The mercury thermometer is invented by German physicist Daniel Gabriel Fahrenheit.

1772
Carl Scheele discovers oxygen, but his findings are published only after Joseph Priestley discovers it independently in 1774.

•1400 •1500 1600• 1700•

1669
German alchemist Hennig Brand obtains phosphorus by boiling 50 buckets of urine!

1766
English chemist Henry Cavendish discovers hydrogen, which he calls "inflammable air".

1789
Antoine Lavoisier compiles a list of elements. It includes hydrogen, zinc, oxygen, nitrogen, phosphorus, mercury, and sulfur.

1436
Printing press

In Germany, Johannes Gutenberg builds a printing press that uses moveable type. The type is made of a lead, tin, and antimony alloy. Suddenly it is much easier to spread scientific ideas.

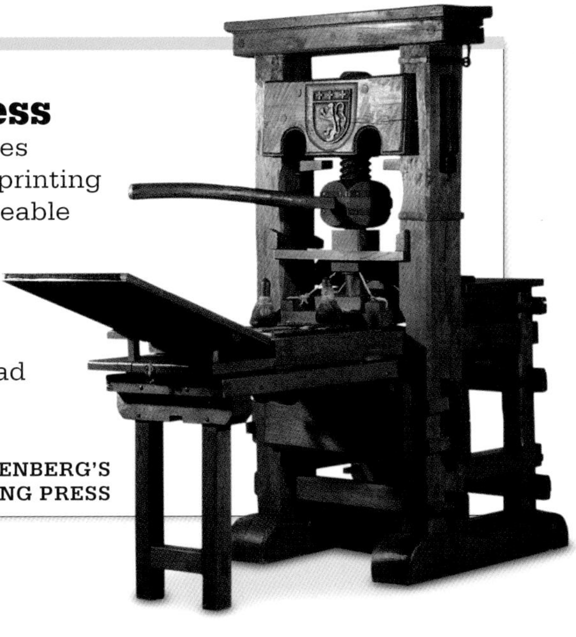

REPLICA OF GUTENBERG'S PRINTING PRESS

1800
Volta's battery

Alessandro Volta, an Italian nobleman, invents the first battery. It provides a new way of splitting up compounds using electricity.

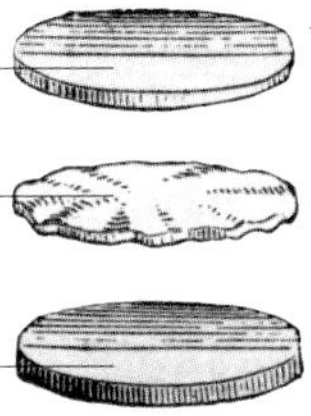
Copper disc
Paper disc soaked in saltwater
Zinc disc

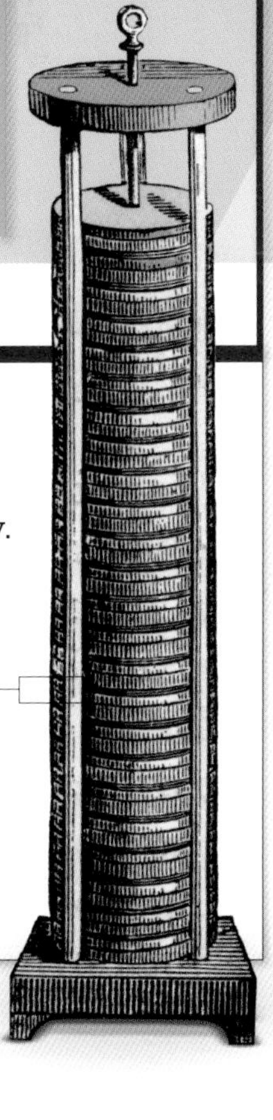

VOLTA'S BATTERY

New ideas [Technology

HUMPHRY DAVY
English champion
Invented: miner's safety light
Discovered: 6 elements

1807
Electro-chemistry
Humphry Davy uses Volta's battery (see page 101) to split up substances with electricity. In this way, Davy discovers the elements sodium and potassium.

1869
Largest gold nugget
"Welcome Stranger", the largest single gold nugget ever found, is excavated from the ground at Moliagul, in Victoria, Australia.

70 kg
(154 lb) – the weight of gold extracted from "Welcome Stranger" after smelting

1879
Light goes on
American inventor Thomas Edison introduces his filament lamps. The filaments are bamboo threads that have been heated until they turn into carbon.

EDISON'S 1879 FILAMENT LAMP

1805
English schoolteacher John Dalton figures out the link between elements and atoms.

1848
The gold rush at Sutter's Mill, California, attracts 300,000 prospectors thirsty for riches.

•1800 1825• •1850 1875•

1810
In the UK, Peter Durand patents the tin can, made with tinplate steel and sealed with toxic lead.

1828
Swedish chemist Jöns Jakob Berzelius (discoverer of six elements) introduces letters to symbolize elements.

1844
Charles Goodyear, an American inventor, strengthens rubber with sulfur, enabling more durable tyres and shoe soles to be made.

1876
Copper wires used to connect telephones allow the first long-distance calls to be made.

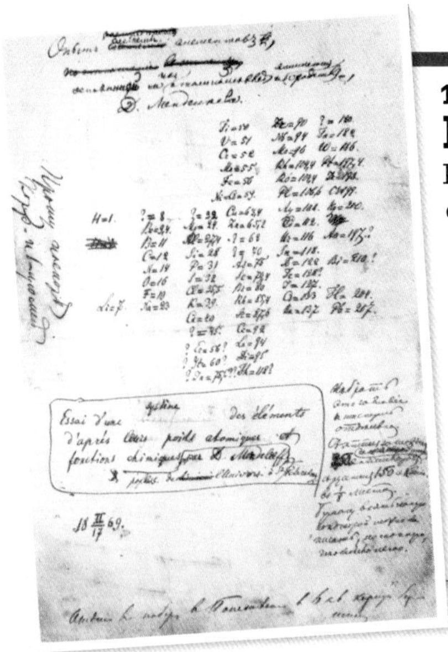

1869
Periodic table
Dmitri Mendeleev, a Russian chemist, produces his first periodic table. Other chemists have identified families of elements but cannot make the 63 known elements fit a pattern. Mendeleev's genius is to leave gaps in his table for undiscovered elements.

MENDELEEV'S FIRST PERIODIC TABLE

58.4 cm
(23 in) – the largest bubblegum bubble ever blown

1888

Chrome yellow

The Dutch artist Vincent van Gogh paints his vibrant Sunflowers series of pictures. The intensity of the colours is made possible by new artificial pigments such as chrome yellow, which is made with the element chromium (see page 57).

SUNFLOWERS, VINCENT VAN GOGH, 1888

1906

Bubble gum

The first bubble gum, Blibber-Blubber, has sulfur in its recipe. It is not successful – it bursts into a sticky mess when blown. Dubble Bubble gum solves the problem in 1928 by including stretchy latex in its ingredients.

GUM BALLS

1886
Coca-Cola is invented by Dr John Pemberton, an Atlanta pharmacist. The drink contains phosphoric acid, a compound of phosphorus.

1898
Scottish chemist William Ramsey discovers the noble gases krypton, neon, and argon.

1900

1900
Waterproof cellophane film is invented by treating plant material with sodium sulfate.

1909–1913
German chemists Fritz Haber and Carl Bosch develop a process to make ammonia by reacting nitrogen with hydrogen.

1912
Physicists Ernest Rutherford and Niels Bohr come up with a new theory of the atom.

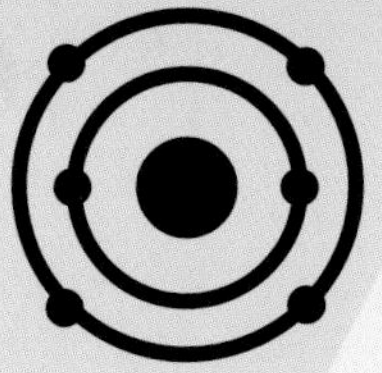

1925

1932
English physicist James Chadwick bombards beryllium with radiation and discovers the neutron.

1898

Radioactivity

Polish-born chemist Marie Curie (see pages 66–67) discovers radioactive polonium and radium with her husband, Pierre, a French scientist, in Paris. She develops a theory of radioactivity that changes the way we think about atoms.

1903

First powered flight

To reduce the weight of their plane, the *Flyer*, the Wright brothers cast its engine block from aluminium. The usual cast-iron block would have been too heavy for takeoff.

THE WRIGHTS' *FLYER*

Creating elements [Adding

1945
Atom bomb
During World War II, the USA develops atomic bombs. The first bomb, made using uranium, is dropped on Hiroshima, Japan, on 6 August. Three days later, a second bomb, which uses plutonium, strikes the city of Nagasaki.

ATOMIC BOMB BLAST

1957
Sputnik I
The first vehicle into space, the satellite *Sputnik I*, is launched by the USSR. It is protected by a heat-resistant shield of aluminium-magnesium-titanium alloy. The shield is just 1 mm (0.04 in) thick, yet very tough.

SPUTNIK I SATELLITE

1935
Synthetic nylon, designed to replace silk, is produced by American chemist Wallace Carothers.

1937
The Hindenburg – the last great hydrogen-filled airship – explodes, killing 35 people (see pages 34–35).

1938
Teflon (PTFE) – a carbon and fluorine compound – is developed. It is used to make non-stick coatings, bearings, sealants, fabrics, and more.

1945

1949
American Willard Libby invents a way of dating ancient objects using radioactive carbon-14.

1952
Einsteinium and fermium are discovered in the debris of the nuclear test of the first hydrogen atomic bomb, "Ivy Mike".

1955
The first super-accurate atomic clock, regulated by caesium atoms, goes on sale.

1959
The popular plastic doll Barbie is put on sale.

GLENN T. SEABORG
American champion
Invented: the actinoid series
Discovered: 10 elements

1951
New elements
While working at the University of California, Berkeley, American chemist Glenn T. Seaborg identifies several new elements that are heavier than uranium. These unstable elements are made in particle accelerators.

1960
Laser
American physicist Theodore Maiman invents the laser, which makes intense light beams. The colour of the light depends on which elements are used in the laser. Argon, for example, gives blue.

LASER LIGHT SHOW

1981
Space shuttle
The space shuttle *Columbia*, the first-ever reusable space vehicle, makes its first flight. The craft is built from aluminium alloy, with titanium alloy used for the engine housing. The space shuttle's detachable boosters are encased in steel.

SPACE SHUTTLE READY FOR ITS FIRST LAUNCH

2004
Diamond in the sky
The Universe's biggest diamond is detected in the core of a white dwarf star in the constellation Centaurus. This lump of crystallized carbon is 3,000 kilometres (1,865 miles) wide and weighs about 2.5 thousand trillion trillion tonnes.

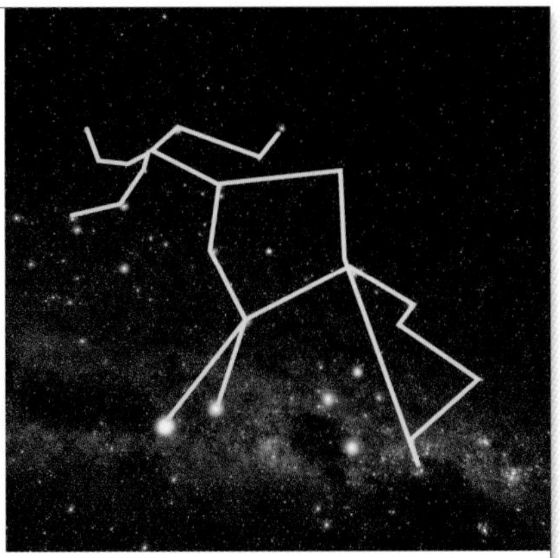

THE CONSTELLATION CENTAURUS

By comparison, the largest uncut diamond ever found on Earth weighed 621 g (22 oz.)

1966
The synthetic fibre Kevlar, invented by American chemist Stephanie Kwolek, is patented. Five times stronger than steel, it is made of carbon, hydrogen, nitrogen, and oxygen.

1965 • 1975 • 1985 • 1995 • 2005 • 2015

1965
American James T. Russell patents the compact disc (CD). It records data on a reflective layer of aluminium.

1967
An artificial nylon turf (a hydrogen-carbon-nitrogen compound) is patented in the USA.

1983
Motorola's DynaTAC 8000X is the first personal, handheld mobile phone to go on sale. It has a nickel-vanadium battery.

1999
The world's largest silver and lead mine is established at Cannington, Queensland, Australia.

2011
Elements 114 and 116 are added to the periodic table.

1961
Microchip
In Texas, Jack Kilby makes the first microchip – a slice of germanium carrying tiny, linked electronic components. It enables electronic devices to be made much smaller.

MAGNIFIED VIEW OF MICROCHIP SURFACE

1991
Carbon nanotubes
Sumio Iijima, a Japanese physicist, discovers a new form of carbon – tiny tubes 50,000 times thinner than human hairs. These nanotubes are super-strong and have useful electrical properties.

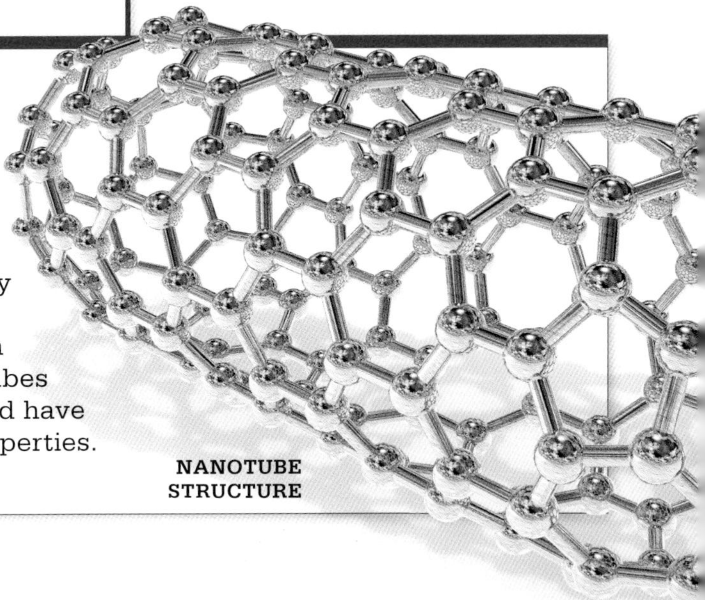

NANOTUBE STRUCTURE

Alkali
A substance that dissolves in water and neutralizes acids; the chemical opposite of an acid. Alkali metals are commonly found combined in alkaline compounds.

Alkaline
Having the properties of an alkali.

Allotrope
One of two or more distinct forms of the same element that have different properties but are the same state of matter (solid, liquid, or gas). Diamond and graphite are solid allotropes of carbon.

Alloy
A metallic mixture made of two or more elements. Alloys include bronze, solder, and steel.

Alpha particle
A particle consisting of two protons and two neutrons that is released when the nucleus of a radioactive atom decays.

Atmosphere
The layer of mixed gases surrounding planet Earth.

Atom
A tiny particle of matter, consisting of protons, neutrons, and electrons. Atoms are the smallest particles that can take part in a chemical reaction.

Atomic bomb
An immensely powerful bomb that releases energy by splitting the nuclei of atoms in a chain reaction.

Atomic clock
A super-accurate clock that uses the natural vibrations of atoms (such as caesium) to count time. Atomic clocks are used to keep the official time standard and to control GPS satellites.

Atomic number
The number of protons in the nucleus of an atom. Elements are arranged on the periodic table in order of increasing atomic number.

Beta particle
A fast-moving electron that is released by the decay of a radioactive nucleus.

Boiling point
The point at which a liquid, when heated, stops increasing in temperature and starts to evaporate, or turn into a gas.

Burning
A type of reaction, between a substance and oxygen in the air, that gives off heat and flames.

Carbohydrate
A chemical compound made up of carbon, hydrogen, and oxygen. Many carbohydrates, including sugar and starch, are vital to life.

Catalyst
A material that helps a chemical reaction take place. The catalyst itself is not used up or changed by the reaction.

Chain reaction
A nuclear reaction that splits the nucleus of an atom, releasing neutrons that then split the nuclei of other atoms. Controlled chain reactions are used in nuclear power stations; uncontrolled chain reactions create nuclear explosions.

Compound
A substance made of two or more elements bonded, or linked, together chemically.

Conductor
A material that allows heat or electricity to pass through it.

Corrosion
The chemical breakdown of the surface of a metal.

Density
A measure of how heavy an object feels. The more weighty the atoms or the more tightly packed they are, the denser the object is.

Distillation
The process of heating a liquid mixture to separate its components. Each component is boiled off at a different temperature, and its gas condenses separately.

DNA
The double spiral-shaped molecule found in the nucleus of every one of the cells in a living body. This special molecule contains all the genetic instructions the body needs to grow and develop. *DNA* stands for *deoxyribonucleic acid*.

Electron
A negatively charged particle that orbits, or moves around, the nucleus of an atom.

Electronic
Relating to electrons. Electronics is the scientific investigation of how electrons move through materials.

Enamel
The tough layer that forms the outer coating of teeth.

Fluorescent
Able to emit light when an electric current passes through a noble gas. Low-energy lightbulbs are fluorescent.

Fossil
The preserved remains or trace of a dead plant or animal.

Fossil fuel
Fuel such as coal, crude oil, or gas, made from the remains of dead plants and animals. When fossil fuels burn, they combine with oxygen and release their stored carbon as carbon dioxide gas.

Fusion
The process that creates a new element by joining the nuclei of atoms.

Gamma ray
A very high-frequency wave of electromagnetic energy released from the nucleus of an atom.

Gas
A state of matter in which the

Element with the highest boiling point: rhenium 5,596°C (10,105°F)

Glossary

atoms are free to move around, enabling the substance to fill any container in which it is placed.

Glucose
The simplest form of sugar. Glucose in food is broken down by the body to release energy.

GPS
A satellite system that involves more than 30 satellites orbiting Earth and tells users their exact location and the correct time. *GPS* stands for *Global Positioning System*.

Half-life
The time it takes for half of the atoms in a sample of a radioactive element to decay.

Hydrocarbon
A compound containing mainly carbon and hydrogen. Most hydrocarbons are found in crude oil.

Impurity
Anything that contaminates or reduces the purity of a substance.

Infrared
Relating to low-frequency waves of electromagnetic energy. Infrared radiation is felt as heat.

Laser
An intense, focused beam of light used for communications, cutting, welding, surgery, astronomy, and much more. *Laser* stands for *Light Amplification by Stimulated Emission of Radiation*.

Liquid
A state of matter between solid and gas. A liquid can flow, and it will always take the shape of its container. Its atoms or molecules settle to form a surface.

Magnet
A substance or object that attracts iron, cobalt, nickel, and their alloys.

Element with the highest melting point: carbon 3,186°C (5,767°F)

Magnetic
Able to act as a magnet.

Malleable
Able to be bent, shaped, and worked without breaking.

Matter
Any substance that has mass, meaning that it exerts a downward force on Earth. Matter is made up of atoms and can exist in three different states – solid, liquid, or gas.

Melting point
The point at which a solid, when heated, stops increasing in temperature and starts turning into a liquid.

Meteorite
A rock that falls to Earth from space.

Mineral
A naturally occurring solid compound whose atoms are ordered in crystal patterns. Many rocks are made of minerals.

Molecule
A substance made of more than one atom chemically bonded, or linked, together.

Molten
In a liquified state due to heat.

Nebula
A cloud of gas and dust in space.

Neutron
A particle that has no electrical charge, slightly bigger than a proton. There are neutrons in the nuclei of all atoms except those of hydrogen.

Nuclear
Relating to the nucleus, or core, of an atom.

Ore
A rock or mineral that contains a valuable or useful substance.

Osteoblast
A cell that makes new bone.

Particle
A tiny part, such as an atom or molecule, that makes up matter. Atoms themselves are made up of even smaller particles called protons, neutrons, and electrons.

Particle accelerator
A machine that uses magnets to accelerate particles around a track. Collisions between the particles release huge amounts of energy and sometimes create new particles or new elements.

Periodic table
A table of all the elements, arranged in order of increasing atomic number and grouped into "families" of elements that have similar properties.

Photosynthesis
The process by which plants use the energy in sunlight to make food from carbon dioxide and water. Oxygen is released as a waste product of photosynthesis.

Pigment
A substance, often a solid powder, that gives colour to paint.

Pollution
The contamination of the environment by harmful substances.

Pressure
The force exerted by a gas on the walls of its container. Air pressure is the force exerted by the atmosphere on Earth's surface.

Property
A characteristic quality of a material or substance.

Proton
A positively charged particle found in the nucleus of an atom.

Radiation
Alpha and beta particles, or intense bursts of energy such as gamma rays, emitted by the nucleus of a radioactive atom.

Radioactive
Emitting nuclear radiation.

Radioactive decay
The natural break-up of atomic nuclei in radioactive elements.

Reaction
A process in which an element or compound combines chemically with another.

Reactive
Likely to react chemically.

Rust
A type of corrosion that happens when iron comes into contact with oxygen and water.

Salt
A compound formed when an acid and an alkali react. Table salt, sodium chloride, is one example.

Semiconductor
A material whose electrical conductivity is between that of a metal and a nonmetal. Semiconductors are often made of metalloid compounds.

Smelting
Extracting metal from its ore by heating the ore in a furnace.

Solid
A state of matter in which the atoms or molecules maintain a rigid shape.

Supernova
A huge explosion that takes place when a star has used up all of its fuel and collapses.

The most expensive elements are synthetic – plutonium can cost 100 times more than gold

GALENA (LEAD ORE)

Synthetic
Created artificially. Synthetic elements do not occur naturally on Earth. They are made inside nuclear reactors and particle accelerators.

Tissue
A collection of living cells inside the human body. Muscle is an example of body tissue.

Toxic
Harmful to living things.

Unreactive
Unlikely or unable to react chemically.

X-ray
A high-frequency wave of electromagnetic energy released from outside the nucleus of an atom.

Index

R

S

T

U

V

W

X

Y

Z

PHOTOGRAPHY

1: John Foxx/Getty Images; 2–3: NASA; 6b: Charles O'Rear/Corbis; 7tl: NASA; 7tlc: Scott Dunn/Getty Images; 7trc: Paul Hardy/Corbis; 7r: Time & Life Pictures/Getty Images; 8–9: Javier Trueba/MSF/Photo Researchers, Inc.; 10–11: Yagi Studio/Getty Images; 12tc: J. Hester, A. Loll/Caltech/NASA; 12tr: RIA Novosti/Photo Researchers, Inc.; 14–15: Spike Walker/Scholastic; 15tl: Andrew Lambert Photography/Photo Researchers, Inc.; 15tc: Charles D. Winters/Photo Researchers, Inc.; 15tr: Lawrence Migdale/Photo Researchers, Inc.; 15b: Kari Greer/Science Photo Library; 16tl: Motoring Picture Library/Alamy; 19br: Maximilien Brice, CERN/Science Photo Library; 20tr, 20–21: NASA; 21tl: Scholastic; 21tc, 21tr: NASA; 24tl (beryllium): Roberto De Gugliemo/Science Photo Library; 24tl (sodium): grafvision/Shutterstock; 24cl (potassium): Andrew Lambert Photography/Science Photo Library; 24cl (calcium): Charles D. Winters/Photo Researchers, Inc.; 24c (titanium): Visuals Unlimited/Corbis; 24cl (francium): Astrid & Hanns-Frieder Michler/Photo Researchers, Inc.; 24cl (radium), 24bc (uranium): Joel Arem/Photo Researchers, Inc.; 24br (plutonium): Photo Researchers; all other images on page 24: images of elements.com; 25tl (gold): Dirk Wiersma/Photo Researchers, Inc.; 25tc (phosphorus): Charles D. Winters/Photo Researchers; 25tc (sulfur): Ted Kinsman/Photo Researchers, Inc.; 25tr (chlorine gas); 25c (arsenic): Charles D. Winters/Photo Researchers, Inc.; 25c (tin): Gary Cook/Visuals Unlimited, Inc./Gettyimages; 25cl (platinum): E.R.Degginger/Science Photo Library; 25cl (mercury): Cordelia Molloy/Science Photo Library; 25c (lead): Hermann Eisenbeiss/Photo Researchers, Inc.; all other images on page 25: images of elements.com; 26tl: Charles D. Winters/Photo Researchers, Inc.; 26 tc: iStockphoto; 26tr: CGI Backgrounds.com/Getty Images; 30tr: Grafvision/Shutterstock; 30cl: Martyn Goddard/Corbis; 30cr: Charles D. Winters Photo Researchers, Inc.; 30bl: Astrid & Hanns-Frieder Michler/Photo Researchers, Inc.; 30br: Science Source/Photoresearchers, Inc.; 31: Vaughan Fleming/Photo Researchers, Inc.; 32l, 32br: NASA; 33 tl: Crown Copyright/Health & Safety Laboratory/Science Photo Library; 33c: DLR Publicity; 33bl, 33cbl: iStockphoto; 33cbr: Bill Brand/Alamy; 33br: Planetary Visions Ltd/Science Photo Library; 34–35: Bettmann/Corbis; 36tl: Joel Arem/Photo Researchers, Inc.; 36tc: Warut Roonguthai; 36tr: Ashley Cooper/Alamy; 36bl: SPL/Photo Researchers, Inc.; 37: Gary Cook, Inc./Visuals Unlimited/Corbis; 38tl: J. Markow/Shutterstock; 38bl: iStockphoto; 38r: 3DClinic/Leigh Russell/Getty Images; 39l: Emely/Corbis; 39tc: Radius Images/Getty Images; 39tr: Pictorial Press Ltd/Alamy; 39c and cr: NASA; 40–41: CGI Backgrounds.com/Getty Images; 42 tc: NASA; 42tr: Time & Life Pictures/Getty Images; 46bl: NASA; 48tl: Donald Nausbaum/Getty Images; 48tr: Tom Grill/Corbis; 48bl: Andrew Syred/Photo Researchers, Inc.; 48bc: Cordelia Molloy/Science Photo Library; 49: Manfred Kage/Science Photo Library; 50–51: Royal Armouries; 52 tl; Dirk Wiersma/Photo Researchers, Inc.; 52 cl: Boltin Picture Library/ Bridgeman Art Library; 52 cr: Donald R. Swartz/Shutterstock; 52 bc: Lebrecht Music and Arts Photo Library/Alamy; 52 br: Pjr Studio/Alamy; 53tl: Jonathan Kitchen/Getty Images; 53tr: Eye of Science/Photo Researchers, Inc.; 53brc: NASA; 53b: Porky Pies Photography/Alamy; 53bc: North Wind Picture Archives/Alamy; 54tr: Photo Researchers, Inc.; 54cl: Pasquale Sorrentino/Photo Researchers, Inc.; 54c: iStockphoto; 54br: AFP/Getty Images; 54–55: Henry K. T. Kaiser/Index Stock/Corbis; 55tr: The Granger Collection, NYC; 55cr: Library of Congress; 56tl: Jean-Daniel Sudres/Hemis/Corbis; 56cl: Visuals Unlimited/Getty Images; 56 br: Time & Life Pictures/Getty Images; 56bl: Scientifica/Getty Images; 56–57 (tubes of paint), 57 tl: Stephen Oliver/Getty Images; 57tr: Cordelia Molloy/Science Photo Library; 57cr: Biophoto Associates/Photo Researchers, Inc.; 57 bcr: Richard Treptow/Photo Researchers, Inc.; 57 br: Photo Researchers, Inc.; 58tl: David Parker/Photo Researchers, Inc.; 58tr: Erich Lessing/Art Resource, NY; 58cl: Wildlife GmbH/Alamy; 58ctl: Martin Bond/Photo Researchers, Inc.; 58cbl: Charles D. Winters/Photo Researchers, Inc.; 58bl: North Wind Picture Archives/Alamy; 58bc: J.L.Images/Alamy; 58cr: AFP/Getty Images; 58br: Mathias Beinling/Alamy; 59tl: GIPhotoStock/Photo Researchers, Inc.; 59bl: iStockphoto; 59c: UrbanEye/Alamy; 59r: Obstando Images/Alamy; 60–61: AFP/Getty Images; 62tr: Olaf Doering/Alamy; 62bl: Russ Curtis/Photo Researchers, Inc.; 62br: uwezi/wikipedia; 63tl: Martin Bond/Photo Researchers, Inc.; 63bc: Science Source/Photo Researchers, Inc.; 63br: Corbis; 64bl: Caltech/S.K.Ulkami; 66–67: Time & Life Pictures/Getty Images; 68tl: NASA/JPL/Cornel University; 68tr: Hannah Gal/Photo Researchers, Inc.; 68cl: Gary Cook/Visuals Unlimited; 68cr: images of elements.com; 68bc: Antony Nettle/Alamy; 68br: images of elements.com; 69: Hermann Eisenbeiss/Photo Researchers, Inc.; 70–71: Photo Researchers, Inc.; 72 tl: Charles D. Winters/Photo Researchers, Inc.; 72cl: Klaus Guldbrandsen/Photo Researchers, Inc.; 72bl: Time Life Pictures/Getty Images; 72c: Ted Kinsman/Photo Researchers, Inc.; 72 tr: Wordpress.com; 72br: Colin Keates/Getty Images; 73: iStockphoto; 74tl: Alexander Tsiaras/Photo Researchers, Inc.; 74tc: 3D4Medical/Photo Researchers, Inc.; 74tr: Tom and Steve/Getty Images; 78tl: Interfoto/Alamy; 78cl: Russell Lappa/Photo Researchers, Inc.; 78cr: GL Archive/Alamy; 78bl: Cordelia Molloy/Science Photo Library; 78br: iStockphoto; 79tl: Dirk Wiersma/Photo Researchers, Inc.; 79tr: Photos 12/Alamy; 79cl: Astrid & Hanns-Frieder Michler/Photo Researchers, Inc.; 79cr: Science Photo Library; 79bl: Joel Arem/Photo Researchers, Inc.; 79cb: AFP/Getty Images; 79b: Marc Hill/Alamy; 80bl: Science Photo Library; 80 bc: Ross Frid/Visuals Unlimited/Corbis; 81: David Taylor/Photo Researchers, Inc.; 82tl: Hcrepin/Wikipedia; 82b: M. I. Walker/Photo Researchers, Inc.; 83tr: Kari Greer/Science Photo Library; 83c: John Warden/Monsoon/Photolibrary/Corbis; 84bl: Roger Harris/Photo Researchers, Inc.; 85tr: 3D4Medical/Photo Researchers, Inc.; 86–87: Quinn Rooney/Getty Images; 88tl: iStockphoto; 88tr: Lester V. Bergman/Corbis; 88cl: Corbis Flirt/Alamy; 88cr: foodfolio/Alamy; 88–89: Paul Souders/Corbis; 89tl: Rebecca Hale/Getty Images; 89br; Steve Dunwell/Getty Images; all other images in box on page 89: iStockphoto; 90tl: istockphoto; 90bl: Omikron/Photo Researchers, Inc.; 90–91: Frans Lanting/Corbis; 91tr: NASA; 92 tl: Perennou Nuridsany/Photo Researchers, Inc.; 92bl: Tom and Steve/Getty Images; 92tr: Yukimasa Hirota/Getty Images; 92tr: Yukimasa Hirota/A. Collection/Gettyimages; 92bc: Charles D. Winters/Science Photo Library; 93: Pascal Goetgheluck/Photo Researchers, Inc.; 94tc: Paul Hardy/Corbis; 94bl: Car Culture/Corbis; 94bc: pslawinski/wikipedia; 94br: sspopov/bigstockphoto; 95: Phillip Evans/Visuals Unlimited/Corbis; 96–97: Peter Essick/Aurora Photos/Corbis; 98tl: George Bernard/Photo Researchers, Inc.; 98tc: Dirk Wiersma/Photo Researchers, Inc.; 98tr: Detlev van Ravenswaay/Photo Researchers, Inc.; 100tl: Pascal Goetgheluck/Photo Researchers, Inc.; 100bl: Science Photo Library/Photo Researchers; 100bc: Dirk Wiersma/Photo Researchers, Inc.; 100cr: The Trustees of the British Museum/Art Resource, NY; 101tl: Sheila Terry/Photo Researchers, Inc.; 101c: SPL/Photo Researchers, Inc.; 101tr: Library of Congress/Science Photo Library; 101bc: Scala/White Images/Art Resource, NY; 101br: Sheila Terry/Photo Researchers, Inc.; 102tl: Sheila Terry/Photo Researchers, Inc.; 102tr: © Science and Society/SuperStock; 102bl: SSPL via Getty Images; 103tc: (painting) Christie's Images/Corbis; 103tc (frame of painting): Klaus Hackenberg/Corbis; 103tr: Bon Appetit/Alamy; 103bl: Science Source/Photo Researchers, Inc.; 103br: Science Museum/Science & Society Picture Library; 104tl: Chris Bjornberg/Photo Researchers, Inc.; 104tr: Detlev van Ravenswaay/Photo Researchers, Inc.; 104bl: Omikron/Photo Researchers, Inc.; 104br: Wolfgang Kaehler/Alamy; 105tl: Roger Ressmeyer/Corbis; 105c: iStockphoto; 105tr: NASA/JPL–Caltech E. Churchwell/University of Wisconsin, Madison; 105bl: Astrid & Hanns-Frieder Michler/Photo Researchers, Inc.; 105br: Laguna Design/Photo Researchers, Inc.; 108: Hermann Eisenbeiss/Photo Researchers, Inc.

ARTWORK

12tl, 16–17c, 18, 42tl, 47: Tim Loughead/Precision Illustration; all other artwork: Scholastic.

SPECIAL PHOTOGRAPHY

28–29: Jose Lasheras; 30tl: Gary Ombler; 44–45: Jose Lasheras; 48tc: Gary Ombler; 76–77: Jose Lasheras; 80tc, 80tr: Gary Ombler; 92cr (three images of flower in test tube): Jose Lasheras.

The publisher would like to thank Andrew Szydio and Highgate School, London for their assistance in setting up the experiments on pages 28–29, 44–45, 76–77, 92cr, and Mark Richards for his design assistance.

COVER

Front cover: (background) iStockphoto; (diamond) Sebastian Kaulitzki/Alamy; (airship) iStockphoto; (sulfur) Andrew Lambert Photography/Science Photo Library; (neon) Pslawinski/Wikimedia Commons; (smart phone) iStockphoto; (robot) Charles Taylor/Shutterstock. Back cover: (chemical reaction) Charles D. Winters/Photo Researchers, Inc.; (crystals) ©Scientifica/Visuals Unlimited, Inc. – Amethyst Crystals.

Credits and Acknowledgements